Humanity Inc

Our desperate need of
leadership in today's world

Steve Hurst

Published by New Generation Publishing in 2022

Copyright © Steve Hurst 2022

First Edition

The author asserts the moral right under the Copyright, Designs and Patents Act 1988 to be identified as the author of this work.

All Rights reserved. No part of this publication may be reproduced, stored in a retrieval system or transmitted, in any form or by any means without the prior consent of the author, nor be otherwise circulated in any form of binding or cover other than that in which it is published and without a similar condition being imposed on the subsequent purchaser.

ISBNs:

Paperback: 978-1-80369-503-7
Hardback: 978-1-80369-504-4
Ebook: 978-1-80369-505-1

www.newgeneration-publishing.com

New Generation Publishing

"If so much of what we experience in life is dependent on leadership, it would only seem right that we, as humanity, define what we need from it".

Steve Hurst

To Rob...
 Keep up the fight...
 "no CWE's"!!

Endorsements

"At last! A book that genuinely puts people and the way we treat each other at the very heart of leadership. I have had the privilege of working closely with Steve over many years and witnessed first-hand the skill and authenticity with which he sought to bring the human element and the characteristics that generate narratives that encourage people to thrive and flourish into our coaching and consultancy.

This book represents one of the most authentic approaches to how we look at work and relationships. It challenges conventional thinking, and it speaks from the heart of someone who manifests this thinking in everything they do. I would defy anyone, however experienced, not to find something that provokes interest and consideration of their own style of leadership. It is crammed with strategic examples throughout to support the central and critical tenet - If humanity is to prosper in the future, it needs exceptional leadership. This is an exceptional book which shows many possibilities of how we may achieve this outcome and change the face of leadership for the better."

Andy Vass - Psychologist and Coach

"This is an incredible read based on the premise that rather than lament the dearth of great leadership, we must step up and put humanity and societal good at its very core. Steve's formula cuts through the crap arguing work is a human invention and as such we must unlearn much of what we previously thought of leadership to fundamentally change our paradigm and expectations of it. His writing is steeped in wisdom and authenticity, using philosophy, personal stories, and megatrends to make the case for Humanity Inc and a better world."

Steve Bernard - Founder Connectwell

"Ever since I met Steve through NTL he's been a sincere presence and guide. Sincere in the Latin sense, meaning 'without wax'. This is who he is, how he leads and how he shares his experiences and insights - straight talking and ever so kind. He paints a vivid picture of how our humanity can show up fully in today's leadership. Creating places where we can turn towards, move through and go beyond the obstacles that prevent us, and others, from becoming our fullest selves. A relevant, practical and vital read for anyone who cares about leading effectively and from love."

Penny Mowberry –
Culture & Organisation Improvement Specialist

"A must read for those in leadership committed to building a better humanity. Driven by a deep personal commitment and leveraging his extensive professional experience, Steve challenges the reader to reflect upon the poor leadership many people are experiencing either in work, or in government and more importantly the leadership we desperately need to ensure humanity's future. With relevant and practical examples Steve positions the Purpose of work with a simple yet powerful model - Do Great, Do Good and Be well – in a Human Centred Leadership model. Through the book Steve provides the tools and encouragement, so that each one of us can take practical steps to become better leaders. The world would certainly be a better place if more people followed this approach."

Jorge Aisa Dreyfus – Executive Vice President, Talent,
Capability & Culture Sage

"This is a great book on leadership thorough and well researched. Having worked with Steve his passion for leadership shouts out from the pages in this inspiring book."

Rob Rave - Creator of Laser 30, Executive Coach &
former Head of Teaming EY

"We need to show up to work differently. In his new book, Humanity Inc, Steve Hurst leads a new way forward by focusing on the ever-increasingly important facets of meaning, growth, belonging and attention."

**Kim Witten PhD –
Transformational Coach and Research Consultant**

"As an experienced leader in business and in the military it was refreshing to read Steve's book, Humanity Inc. Leadership is not about the individual but the people and organisation they serve and Steve brings this out brilliantly. I commend everyone to join the Humanity Club."

**David Bradley –
Key Note Speaker, High Performance and Leadership Consultant**

Acknowledgements

I have been very fortunate; many wonderful people have had an influence in the writing of this book.

To my 'hall of famers' who showed me what exceptional leadership was: Keith Bowden, Frank Mooney, Laura Walker and in fond memory of; Frank Howard, Lee Adams, Ron Herbert, Peter Whiting, Dr Mee-Yan Cheung-Judge and Jack Cleminson, whose memories live on in all that I do.

To friends, clients, coaches and colleagues: Colin Russell, Andy Vass, Danny Hann, Innes Alexander, Adrian Price, Andy Hill, Ian Gregory, Sonia Hudson, Stuart Beech, Seamus Smith, Katrin Evers, Elissa Patrick, Sheryl Miller, Rob Rave, Brent Mattson, Leslie Young, Rayman Som, Frenchie Kessler, Steve Cole, Emma Doran, Martin Walton, Gordian Mothersole, Lorraine Everett, Richard Drury, Amanda Cusdin, Jorge Aisa Dreyfus, Ron Baston, Penny Mowberry, Grace Marshall, Kay Penny, Terri Weithorn, Leanne Bailey, Debbie Wall, Sandy Abraham, Keith Rosen, James Crow, Professor Dan Cable, Dr Jules Goddard and Giles Ford.

To the NTL faculty, and in particular, Cohorts 8 and 9, all the OLA faculty at IMD and fellow learners, and finally The Green Door Team and Emerging World; thank you for all your support and for allowing me the privilege of working and continually learning from and with you over recent years.

Thank you to my wonderful wife, Sherrise, for without your belief in me and continued support and love, this book would not have been published.

This book is dedicated to my late father, for all our conversations over the years on the meaning of 'life and leadership' that I learnt so much from and miss daily.

For Aleena & Darcey -

two special young ladies who deserve better

Introduction

Never in history has humanity been so reliant on leadership. In our world today, the quality of our human experience directly relates to the quality of the leaders leading it. All the problems humanity faces *right now* have been created by leaders and their leadership and it will be the quality of their leadership that will determine whether humanity overcomes them and survives in tomorrow's world.

Whether on the commercial, political or environmental stage, we have witnessed the inability of leadership to create solutions that are right for humanity. Granted, these problems are, by nature, complex and fraught with unknowns, and yet if humanity is to exist and thrive in the future, overcome them we must. We have publicly witnessed a lack of leadership integrity in the business and political world. We have seen leaders divide nations, create conflict and openly flout laws, leading to corruption, disbelief, frustration, hate and an appalling lack of trust in our societies.

Humanity has no global standard by which it defines and measures leadership. That said, through social media, the court of public opinion is positively thriving, with humanity screaming at leaders to *do* and *be better*.

> But what is 'better' and how do leaders 'do it' and how can humanity demand it?

If humanity is to prosper in the future, it needs exceptional leadership. Much has been written about leadership over the years. We have made leadership complicated beyond comprehension. It has become an academic study, with forensic insights in terms of what it should be, when humanity's need for a leader and leadership are fundamental to meeting our needs as humans.

According to Google, right now, there are 15,000 books on leadership in print. I find this bewildering. I have been reading books on leadership since the mid-90s. Over recent years, when reading and researching leadership, it has felt like *déjà vu*. One of the *many* reasons for writing this book is that I had become bored of reading the same old stuff regarding leadership. My hope is that in a world where we currently have a frightening lack of trust in leadership, and genuine divisions and polarities in our societies caused by inadequate leadership, this book will help reinvigorate our view of leadership, what it is in simple terms and how it can better serve humanity because I believe that is the purpose of leadership.

Who's the leader?

Let's put this question to bed early on since there has been much written on the subject of this question even though the answer is simple:

> If your role on this planet has the welfare of others at its core, then you are a leader.

If you apply this definition, then many of us hold 'leadership' roles as many of us impact upon others and affect the way other humans show up in the world. Whether you are in politics, education or commerce, *wherever* you lead, the principles we are going to cover in this book apply to you. They apply because they represent the universal needs of humanity. They are *your* needs too. Carl R. Rogers was quoted as saying, 'that which is most personal is most universal', and this is true in relation to our collective need of leadership.

Simply put, as a leader, we need to meet the needs of humans. Meet only your needs as a leader, and you are failing.

Who am I and what qualifies me to write on the subject of leadership?

In the early 80s, I started my working life as an engineer. At the beginning of my career, I considered myself to be a 'fixer' (and still do). In my early years of work, I moved from the clothing and manufacturing sector into technology. As a qualified electronic engineer, my formative years were spent with Xerox, and it was while working at Xerox I came 'off the tools' and moved into Team Leadership, Management and Management Training and eventually Leadership Development.

When I left Xerox in the late 90s, I moved in to the pharmaceutical and construction sectors, holding senior leadership roles in Organisational Learning and Leadership Development. More recently, I have founded and ran two successful consultancy companies and worked with prestigious companies and clients in the public and private sectors from around the world.

I am passionate about developing exceptional leadership and great places to work and I love what I do. For the past 25 years, my work in the business world has been focused on developing leadership such that it creates a culture of sustainable high performance. Over the past 15 years, at a time when we are witnessing a proliferation in technology, virtual working and opportunities to fully globalise businesses for the benefit of humanity, I have started to see limits in the way we lead. I began to see how this is causing an increase in stress, fatigue and mental health issues never previously recorded in the wider world of work, leading me to become frustrated and anxious at the way we lead organisations across the globe.

Who's this book for?

If, as previously stated, you hold a role that has the welfare of others at its core, then you will benefit from reading this book. The relationship a leader has with their employee whether in the public or private sector is fundamentally the same relationship as one between a teacher and their pupil, a political leader and their constituent, a spiritual leader and their follower. The fundamental human needs in these relationships are the same. My career has been in business, so as we go through the following chapters, the ideas, examples and stories will have a business focus to them; that said, the same human needs apply across the educational, political and spiritual elements of our lives and I suspect you have your own stories to tell on how leadership has impacted you. Our need for exceptional leaders in all walks of life are the same.

We will explore the growing number of organisations that hold humans central to their existence and these organisations succeed because they attract talented people who want to join a cause. These organisations are remembered and experienced as a great place to work; a place that lifted the human spirit rather than crushed it. A place that 'won' and even when it did not win, people became stronger because of the experience. I believe organisations that offer this in the future will have a competitive edge over their rivals and increase value for all involved with the enterprise.

Too many humans globally are suffering today due to work. Suffering through either the work they choose to do, must do, or through the impact that organisations who operate in their regions are having on the communities in which they live in. There is growing discontentment, and as we travel through this book together, I will provide examples of where leadership has failed and where it is 'winning' – in all senses of the word. My aim in writing this book is to provide more of a synthesis of what is going on right now and what needs to change in relation to work and leadership in the future. At the end of this book, I would love you to join The Humanity Club. An online club, the purpose of which will be to share stories of exceptional leadership and the impact it has had on you as a human and the community it provides employment to. I believe the more we promote the leadership we need in the world, the more we can define it and make it a reality.

But first, what's happening now (the abridged version)

As I write this, we are experiencing the COVID pandemic, Russia has invaded Ukraine, Trump incited an insurrection and Johnson has been unceremoniously kicked out of Downing Street and we are facing economic challenges not seen since the 80's. Leadership around the world has two priorities; to reduce economic hardship and to stop people from dying.

On the COVID front, business leaders are now faced with a dilemma: keeping their employees safe, while offering job security and income, but at the same time, the global economy is in peril. Investors and shareholders are now trusting leaders to do what is right. But what *is* right? Is it to lay off staff to limit risk and protect profits and shareholder value, or is it to find ways to secure employment and income so humans survive, and society prospers?

In previous economic boom and bust cycles, it has been accepted that businesses lay off their people through the downs of the profit cycles. *However, this is different — it's a pandemic*. In many ways, COVID has amplified the tough 'people' choices that leaders have been making for decades. Whoever said 'business is *not* personal' was clearly lying! Business is, and always has been, personal. For those leaders out there who spout this well-worn and out of date mantra, 'It's not personal', need to recognise that it's a way of distancing yourself from any unpalatable leadership decisions. In other words, it's a way of exercising a 'conscience lobotomy'.

As I write this, I am adapting to (well, *trying to*) the new ways of 'working from home', although it feels more like I am 'living at work', whilst continually telling myself, friends, employees and loved ones that 'this isn't the new norm'. After all, working totally virtual, with little to no physical and social interaction, whilst watching rising infections and body count figures on the news, not being able to visit, hug and spend time with friends and loved ones, is *not* normal. In reaction to the shamefully sad and needless death of George Floyd, we are also experiencing the worldwide protests of Black Lives Matter and I am left saddened, curious, and worried about our future. I am wondering what leadership lessons will be learnt from this difficult period in our history, whilst being fearful that nothing will be. Over time things will go back to a representation of what was previously normal. Too often time moves on and lessons are forgotten. We will consign this sad and challenging period for us to history and not extract what it can teach us about leadership and humanity in a broader sense.

We have all witnessed the speed at which some businesses have adapted during the pandemic, and in contrast, been shocked by the lack of speed and sheer ignorance of some businesses and governments in critical times when the virus was spreading, to provide adequate care for their people. Hesitation and indecisiveness in leadership clearly kills. We have witnessed the disparity between countries with the resources and infrastructure to be able to vaccinate and care for their people and those that sadly can't or won't. We have witnessed how leaders can, by what they say and do, heal, or in contrast, further divide society. We have also witnessed how ugly and distasteful it is when there is one rule for one, and one rule for another, and where leadership does not provide a role model and align itself to what it mandates to the wider society. We have also watched as leaders in powerful positions lose a sense of perspective and do not listen to those close to them and start to dangerously believe their own hype, leading to extreme statements that initiate irrational behaviour, division and violence.

This period in history could teach us *so* much and yet learning through a period of reflection and review has never worked for humanity. Reflection and a statement of 'hope' will not work. It's just not the way humanity learns. Think of 'the war to end all wars' (stated about WW1) – then less than 21 years later, another 'world war' (WW2) was started. Humanity only learns when the situation and the problem has been clearly defined and solutions found at the time when they are needed.

On a personal level, after a time of isolation and observing how humanity has reacted and adapted to this pandemic, I am hoping that some of the following valuable lessons will be remembered and realised:

- Humanity is born to get along. How we learn and grow is through social interaction. Even though we can work remotely, we are nourished through physical human connection.
- How much we depend on and value our health and care services – and how much we need to invest in and treasure them in the future.
- How much inequalities around the world are brought into uncomfortable focus when all of humanity faces the same challenge.
- For those of us with children of school age, I suspect many of us have a new-found respect for teachers and how they manage to educate our children.
- How much we cherish our personal freedom to go where we want, meet who we want, when we want.
- The societal value of science and its ability to facilitate global research and development in tackling the pandemic and protecting us in the future.

- The need for all countries to work together and the power of collaboration when faced with what appears to be insurmountable challenges.
- How this period has brought out the 'Saints' and the 'Sinners' in the world of business and political leadership and that the 'Sinners' should have *no place* in the world of work (or politics for that matter) in the future.
- Finally, how much we depend on leadership and how much we need great leaders to secure a safer, happier and more prosperous future for all of humanity.

What could this period teach us about leadership?

It's a question that's time has come, and this book will outline a response to this question, based on research, observation and clarity in relation to our human needs.

The idea that the purpose of business is to simply make money is now out of date. If the purpose of business leadership is to create profit and shareholder value, then in the global context in which we live, my contention is it threatens the very health and existence of humanity. Put simply, the health of humanity is reliant on the health of our world's leadership. While the good news from a business perspective is that a growing number of leaders and investment institutions are recognising the opportunity and need for businesses to be more socially aware on issues such as, social advocacy, representation, inclusivity, diversity and environmental measures and ways of working, and we will cover this and the impact on leadership in more detail later in the book.

I am hopeful this book will become a movement for leadership in the 21st century and a call to action for leaders around the world that not only want to create profit, but also want to create iconic organisations that leave a lasting and positive legacy on humanity. I believe humans should be at the very centre of business. Humanity's recent business history has proved that our reliance on technology, our obsession with profit and value, along with the global market and its need for 'competitiveness and winning at any cost', has meant the 'human' has at best been edged out of the equation, or if not, has been shamelessly exploited.

As we go through the book, we will question and explore the purpose of work; we will also review leadership and offer four essential human needs that should be the watermark of leadership in tomorrow's organization.

I'd like to say this book was started when the pandemic was at its height, but the reality is, this book started decades ago and carries the memories of every experience that I have ever had that has lifted, engaged, developed me and made me proud, as well as those that have disengaged, challenged, scarred and disgusted me. Like me, you also carry these experiences. I suspect you can recall memories of working in organisations with leaders you would readily go back to work for, as well as those you wouldn't walk on the same side of the street with.

I am unsure of the genesis to this book. I remember back in the very early 80s, I was at college in Hackney (London), and on one cold and frosty morning commute I saw a faceless civil servant lying down on the bench of a London tube station. He was clutching his briefcase as if his life depended on it, his pale, sweaty, grey face was looking vacantly up for confirmation that his next breath wasn't going to be his last, while humanity rushed past at great speed to their daily appointments. That memory has stayed with me all my life and I often think about what happened to him. Why didn't people stop? Why didn't *I* stop? Perhaps that was the beginning, the time I really started to question; what's the purpose of work? We all seem so busy earning our way through life. What if work was something else, something more valuable to humanity and if it was, what are the implications for leadership? It could also be any number of the following that have inspired me to think about leadership and work differently:

- Daily news reels of the leaders across the globe who exploit humans by either paying the minimum they can and/or through unsafe working conditions and practices cause hurt and misery to many.
- The children I know, who, although they have two parents, grew up only knowing one. Don't get me wrong, we have come a long way from sending children up chimneys, or down mines, at the age of 6, for 10 hours a day, 6 days a week, but whether by choice or circumstance, today's work still tends to deny parents access to their children for similar amounts of time.
- The leadership rhetoric I have heard over the years (and more frequently of late) from organisations that claim to be diverse and inclusive and yet do not have a workforce reflective of their demographic.
- My numerous conversations with people who have worked so hard all their life and yet now wonder how their work has become so meaningless and such a burden.
- The political leaders who seem to think it is right to say one thing publicly and do another thing privately and that the law doesn't apply to them.
- The growing displacement of humanity in Ukraine, simply because of a leader who wants more land.
- The billionaire leaders who still requested their employees benefit from government furlough support packages, while resting up in their tax-free havens with billions in their bank accounts.
- The numerous reports of increased stress, poor mental well-being, low morale and absenteeism and the cost to our global economy, and more broadly, to society.
- The growing gap between a commercial world that functions globally and yet still operates in places

around the world where the basic needs of millions are still not being met.
- The email I received the other day from a renowned international business school that informed me they had 'laid off a valued member' of their staff (our Account Leader) because of the 'widening implications of the pandemic' – only to ask, when would be a good time to call to explore how they can help our leaders adapt, survive and propser through this pandemic. How is it that they could not see the irony of the request, and that perhaps I would rather do business with an international business school that has also adapted, and benefited from, the pandemic *without* laying off staff.
- And finally, it could just be that I have been simply bemused, frustrated and at times, fearful for the future of work and the way it is going to impact humanity with the current standard of leadership at its helm.

Who knows what the reason is; all I know is I have to write and publish this book and my hope is it inspires a leadership to rethink, because I believe humanity is in desperate need of it. You deserve better. The world deserves better.

It has been said many times before that everyone has a book in them, well this is unashamedly mine. This is what I think leadership is and how I think it needs to meet the needs of humanity in tomorrow's world.

Thank you for reading.
Purton, England – December 2021

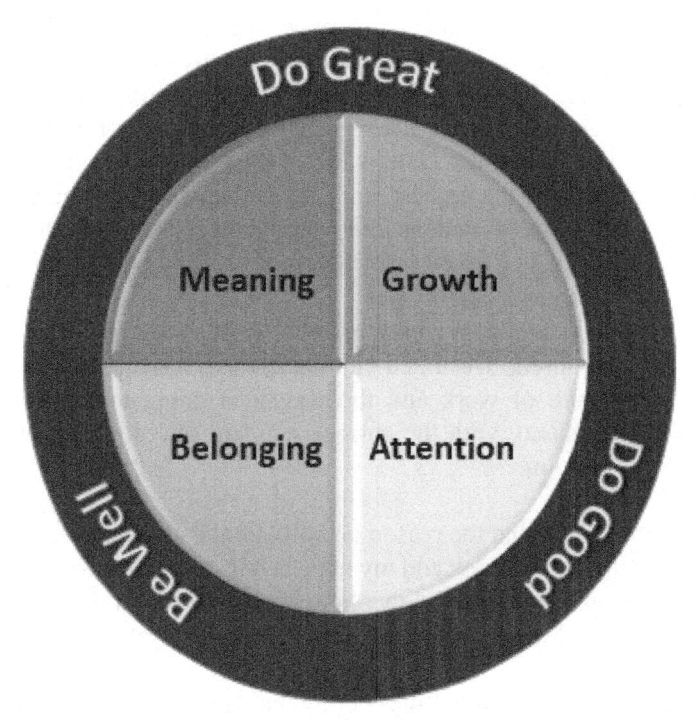

The Purpose of Work – Do Great, Do Good and Be Well
Human Centered Leadership – our FOUR needs

Chapter One: What is the purpose of work?

I remember it well. "You'll look back on your years in school as the best time of your life, you wait till you *have to work for a living*!" Parents have been telling their children that for years (I know mine did) and I hear the same mantra today because for so many, it is sadly true. I say that because if you were an alien and visited Earth to observe 'work', to report back on what it was all about, and you listened to local radio stations (you know, the ones that merrily go on about the fact it is 'nearly the weekend'), TV and read newspapers and listened to and observed people going to work, as well as heard all the reports of numerous corporate and public sector misdemeanours, along with global levels of poverty, famine and disease, what would the conclusion be? The interstellar visitor would have to conclude that the main purpose of work was to make the greater majority of humanity miserable.

True to my parents' prophecy, my first week at work for Burberry in Reading seemed like a year. Up before dawn, home after sundown. At first, I felt like I would shrivel away from lack of sunlight. The weird thing was that, although I did think at the time I was in hell, I very soon began to enjoy my new community of friends. Burberry had been making their famous trench coat in Reading, England, prior to the beginning of the First World War, and generations of families had worked there for many years. At the time I joined its family, some had worked there for more than 40 years. The place felt and sounded like it had a heartbeat because the boiler that created steam for the presses made a rhythmic 'breathing' noise, and I quickly became another vital part of its anatomy. People were enjoying their work and there was pride, purpose and social connection to what they were doing. However, in April 1981, after nearly 70 years in the town, the factory was closed for no clear reason that I can seem to remember, although we later found out they moved it up to Carlisle due to the cheaper labour and lower cost of living. I can still vividly remember hearing, seeing and feeling the pain of taking work away from people. People, who for years, had been loyal and committed to Burberry, now found themselves with no purpose for getting out of bed in the morning.

Work is a human invention which I think needs to change. Looking at the history of work, the industrial revolution was only 150 years ago, the birth of digital technology only 40 years ago and globalisation a mere 25 years ago, and although technology has advanced massively over the past 40 years, as humans, we have struggled to keep up. We seem overly preoccupied with predicting the future skills needed in the workplace and yet we were not able to predict them in the past and we are not able to predict them today. Since the 80s, superpowers have changed; the Cold War has ended, the internet is now semantic and prolific, technology is everywhere and never in our human history did we have so much going for us; that was until 2008! I am a lay person when it comes to the commentary on that part of our history, but here is my take: with our investments, the financial institutions, driven by a level of greed and the desire to reach certain bonus targets, seemed to have gambled with our money and lost, while the governments then globally bailed the banks and financial institutions out with the money we paid as taxes, and as a result, we now have increased taxes and lower government service levels due to paying back the money they loaned the banks. Everyone was looking for someone to blame and yet nobody was seemingly guilty of causing the crisis. It would seem few predicted it happening and we sleepwalked our way into it. Where was the moral and ethical leadership when humanity needed it the most?

> It would seem Peter Drucker was right; work is a place where intelligent people, do awful things to others, with good intentions.

Our leadership mindset is stuck in the 19th century. In work today, 9 to 5 is still the order of the day and so is 'turning up' for work in an office, even though organisations did not crash when employees went virtual due to the pandemic. Even COVID hasn't led to people working wherever and whenever they can and want to because the birth of 'hybrid' working is all about still bringing people into offices, whether they like it or not, mainly for just a few days a week. We are leading the human much like we did machinery back in the 19th century. With machinery, we had the ability to control its efficiency with a level of conformity and this is still the mantra at the heart of many businesses today, i.e., control, conformity and efficiency. With machinery, we were able to increase the speed and therefore create greater efficiency and we are doing (and have been doing for some time) the same with humans today. How many of us are in, or have experienced, the **'impossible job'**, where you don't have enough resources, or enough time, to do what is expected of you? That's a machinery mindset applied to the human. The more you give 'it' to do, the more efficient the 'human' becomes and therefore, the more your business prospers. Thus, we are at an all-time high in terms of stress, fatigue and burnout in business. Our human needs for meaning, growth, belonging and attention have been edged out of the relationship we have with work to the detriment of humanity. Businesses now compete to hire the smartest and yet a job is no longer for life and has not been for years. In a world that has changed hugely with the advent of the dot-com economy and is set to change even more radically in the future as we put this pandemic behind us, now is the time to re-think the purpose of work. We now need to re-purpose work, and this has implications for leadership and how we lead and organise work around the most precious of commodities, the human.

The Awakening

With the recent advances in technology and the proliferation of globalization, work has been fully global in the last few decades. This raises some interesting observations and dilemmas about how leaders operate globally; while the evidence appears to suggest that we are still trying to navigate this new world order. For example, in the early 90s, businesses started to consider outsourcing into 'low cost' centres, lowering their operating margins by (some would say) 'exploiting' lower salary-based countries. These then turned in to 'high-value' centres, which seemed a more palatable term and yet had the same intent, i.e., to exploit low-cost labour. I was once told that 'good business is only "good" when both parties prosper' and you could argue that even with these 'low-cost' or 'high-value' centres, both parties *actually do prosper*, but in a world where there is vividly widening inequality, we must tread carefully. Ultimately, the minimum offering and benefit in this business exchange is employment, but is that enough? There are business leaders out there who park their companies from one low-cost region to the next (or one tax haven to the next) in a never-ending attempt to keep their costs low and margins high. The argument that businesses have a fiduciary responsibility to ensure they gain the maximum share value by reporting healthy tax returns from countries that allow them to do that is weakening. Business and the act of commerce being devoid of any global ethics will change. It is my contention that, in the future, these organisations will be viewed much the same way as slavery and workhouses are today – out of date, out of touch and out of order.

We use the term 'VUCA' to describe a business world that is volatile, uncertain, complex and ambiguous, and yet I think this acronym understates the reality. I see a world of work that is arguably much more underrepresented, unbalanced, under-nourished and unfair than ever before.

To compound matters further, we have schooled and educated leaders to find every angle to compete and win commercially, regardless of the impact at a human or societal level, and yet business and the wider world's economy and societal standards are intrinsically linked. If business is global, then we cannot continue to rely solely on local governments to address local issues; surely those businesses that operate globally are also responsible for the wealth and health of the societies in which they operate. Organisations that understand this link and align their business model and strategy to something bigger, will be the ones that create greater overall value and wealth for humanity in the 21st century. This isn't a new idea, just an idea that I believe has now come of age.

> There is no wealth but life. Life, including all its powers of love, of joy, and of admiration. That country is the richest which nourishes the greatest numbers of noble and happy human beings; that man is richest, who, having perfected the functions of his own life to the utmost, has also the widest helpful influence, both personal, and by means of his possessions, over the lives of others.
>
> **John Ruskin, Unto This Last**

Aristotle possibly stated it more succinctly: 'What is the essence of life? To serve others and to do good.' *This* is the purpose of leadership.

For some time now, humanity has underestimated the impact that work and leadership has had on us as humans. Our attention has been narrowed by an unhealthy focus on levels of service, cost, margin, revenue, profit and value. Yes, it's about winning and profit; yes, it's about market share; yes, it's also about shareholder value and wealth creation; and *yes, of course* it's about world-class products and services; and yet to focus solely on numerical measures of success, to the detriment of the health and wealth of humanity in tomorrow's world, will, I believe, be corporate suicide.

Why is humanity's overall quality of life *so* dependent on simply the value of a 'share' and the buoyancy of global markets?

Work's original intention

Perhaps a conveniently forgotten fact about Adam Smith, arguably the father of modern-day capitalism, is that, back in the 18th century, he did not believe, or intend for, his view of capitalism to be one of growth without equality. They say few saw the crash of 2008 coming, but perhaps those that did had heeded Adam Smith's observations that countries with profits are 'always highest in the countries which are going fastest to ruin'. His view of capitalism is often thought to be one of pure self-interest; however, in *The Theory of Moral Sentiments,* he had a more sceptical approach to self-interest as a driver of behaviour:

> How selfish soever man may be supposed, there are evidently some principles in his nature, which interest him in the fortune of others, and render their happiness necessary to him, though he derives nothing from it except the pleasure of seeing it.
>
> **Adam Smith**

It's perhaps no surprise that although the early days of capitalism saw the growth of many profit-driven companies, it also saw the creation of many institutions that started to support and tackle inequality and societal issues of humanity in the day. For example, here in the UK, the industrial era saw the birth of philanthropy and such well-known charities as Barnardo's (1866), who fight against the cruelty and neglect of children, the RSPCA (The Royal Society for the Prevention of Cruelty to Animals) (1824), Battersea Dogs Home (1860), and even Almshouses (low-cost community housing) go back to the year of 990, although today's version of the Association of Alms Houses was formed in 1946. These, and other charities like them, globally rely on funding from the public and private sectors.

Certainly, billions are given to charities each year through philanthropic donations, not to mention the donations to the International Monetary Fund (IMF) and the World Bank. For instance, The Giving Pledge was started by Warren Buffet, Melinda French Gates and Bill Gates to encourage billionaires to donate 50% of their wealth either in their lifetime, or in their will, to worthy causes.

In a recent report that was summarised by *Forbes* magazine, the Chief Executives for Corporate Purpose (CECP), a coalition of more than 200 of the world's largest companies, recently released its annual survey of corporate philanthropy and employee engagement in 2018 (Giving in Numbers). This year, 250 multi-billion-dollar companies with aggregate revenues of more than $7.9 trillion participated in the survey[1]. As per the previous year, 92% of surveyed companies offered at least one kind of gift-matching programme to their employees, with 78% offering two (typically an annual workplace giving campaign and a year-round programme).

> To donate such amounts is a tremendous gift to humanity, but is gifting what's most needed?

The unsaid here is how many of those businesses' philanthropic donations are buying a conscience that posits, 'we're doing our bit'. When the line between business rules and morality becomes blurred (as it often does), I wonder whether accepting business donations compounds the issues relating to moral leadership and thus, allowing businesses to continue to go about their work in a world free from guilt. This may sound cynical, but I think donating is the minimum expectation we should hold of successful businesses that operate globally. Monetary donations do help, but businesses having their people working and supporting in more places around the world that need it, not only helps overcome the societal challenges, but it also helps build more awareness of diversity and a commitment of humanity to see and address the wider issues we are facing. Philanthropy needs to *do* more, not just donate more.

> What if work was created from a different model, where the lines between work and its impact on society were blurred?

The purpose of this book is not to directly challenge the fundamental ideology of capitalism. Other far more intelligent people than me are rightly conversing and building control mechanisms in line with that agenda. The purpose of this book is to simply challenge the current purpose of work and its broader impact on the health and wealth of humanity and offer a leadership approach that is not only good for business but also good for humanity.

There is no doubt that, because of this pandemic, work will change. Nobody can truly predict the way work will change but it will certainly have implications for leadership and the way work is structured. It will also have implications on the footprint leaders leave on the world going forward. I say this because there are three forces for change that are simultaneously coming together, and they are questioning and demanding a different relationship between humans and work.

The widening impact of society on work

In the public and private sector, we have seen a growth in Environmental, Social and Governance (ESG) investment over the past few decades, and thankfully, this is only set to continue, with currently over USD 17.5 trillion globally being invested[2]. We have also seen major finance investors begin to consciously invest their portfolios in sustainable businesses, and this also is only set to grow.

As well as the growing ESG agenda and associated investment patterns that are influencing change, there are other influential factors that, because of this pandemic, are going to change how we experience work.

The Shifting Age Demographic

Some journalists have termed the global decline in children being born as 'jaw dropping', and have predicted the current population boom will reach a peak in 2064 at 9.7 billion, then fall to 8.8 billion by the end of this century.
Although we will have fewer youngsters coming into work, all the research is indicating we will also have an ageing workforce globally. Less than 20% of the work population in the 1950s was above the age of 50. In 2000, it was 60%, and it is expected to grow. This is mainly due to the poor performance of pension funds and people needing to supplement their retirement income. These people do not want to work long hours and become a slave to the corporate rhythm; these people, who are in later life, tend to look for opportunities that fit in with their lifestyle and income needs.

Along with a shifting age demographic, children have, more recently, seen their parents working long hours, coming home drained, exhausted and miserable from their day at work; these parents are unknowingly offering this perception as 'work', and demonstrating what their children can expect when they leave school, college or university.

You only have to look at our bestseller bookshelves for stark reminders of today's reality: The *One Minute Bedtime Story* and *The 30-minute Father* are books that have topped the book charts in recent years. And although the time spent with family and friends differs across the globe, on average, a child in the UK spends just 5 hours with parents every week[3], or 42 minutes a day, which is 5 minutes more than the US at 37 minutes per day[4]. What has happened to our lives and what effect is this having on our society? It seems that we have become money-rich, time-poor, or sadly, in too many circumstances, just time-poor.

These children are now coming into work and rightly demanding a different relationship with work, due to what they have experienced and are seeing in the world. They have witnessed the strain, burden and neglect work can create in a family, they have been born into a world where injustice, misery and inequality are clearly evident through the social channels available to them. This generation have also been brought up as digital natives, meaning they are digitally savvy and able (and all too willing) to share their views about what is good and not so good in their lives, and this includes work.

The continuous evolution of technology

These 'digital natives' are now the generation coming into work; it is rather sobering to say that those of us who were born prior to 1982 had limited access to PCs and so we have had to 'migrate' to the digital age and are therefore called 'digital migrants'.
In the context of work, here are some interesting facts about digital natives:

- With everything at their fingertips, they are used to getting something now.
- They are used to sharing and have a high need for connection through technological mediums.
- They are often very good at multitasking and are looking for challenging and stimulating work environments.
- The word 'career' is viewed as a plural.
- Much like playing a PC game, they are used to going up to the 'next level' when they have done what is expected and have low tolerance for organisations that don't offer such career opportunities.

- Also, like a PC game, if work's enjoyable, they'll stick at it; if not, they'll move on.
- They require and demand fewer boundaries between work and play.
- They are conscious of social issues, and many will take an activist position in tackling an issue if it is either close to their hearts, or socially, there is a large movement they can join and gain a sense of belonging to.
- Many need work to have a meaning wider than the purpose of the work itself.

As with all of the 'next' generations, they want to change things and, in doing so, naturally challenge the status quo. With the advent of the 'semantic' web in 2003, we can all now ask the internet any question and have an answer immediately. This means that with the advent of Artificial Intelligence (AI) and Machine Learning (ML), knowledge is fast becoming virtual and this means that the capabilities valued by work will shift to 'non-cognitive skills', i.e., empathy, curiosity and people-centred activities like collaboration, team working, problem-solving, reasoning and getting things done through others etc.

The best current example of how the semantic web influences our lives is through the likes of Apple's Siri and Amazon's Alexa. Although this technology is still in its infancy (if Siri hears 'Syria' mentioned on the news in our household, it springs into action, only to be told to 'stand down'), it offers knowledge at the point of need and can automate the most basic of human tasks. This, coupled with the sheer amount of information available on the web, has meant that knowledge is becoming far less valuable now than in previous history. We once lived in a world where knowledge was power, and yet with technology advancements, knowledge itself has become ubiquitous, and the more knowledge you can *share* through social platforms, the more popular and valuable you become:

where once we held on to knowledge to retain a sense of our own value, we now give it away.

With the advent and proliferation of social platforms and the technology now to interact anytime and anywhere, most of us can now work remotely. The myth of putting your feet up while 'working from home' has been dispelled for many. With people who can work from home now doing so, and along with it with, little to no commute time, we have found that productivity will remain high because we humans ultimately don't like to let people down.

Technology is shaping the way we work, but at the same time causing no end of challenges for companies globally, that are struggling to not only keep up with the latest technology trends, but are also trying to ensure those tech and system investments are being maximised by the people who are using them, many of whom are not digital natives. The pursuit of digital fluency in organisations is becoming a major challenge for many leaders.

At the start of the pandemic, many business leaders were certain they would no longer require offices. Even Google and Twitter, who were early adopters of the 'we are never going back to the office' campaign, are now softening their stance and in doing so, will mostly likely end up using a hybrid work model, where the constituent parts of the organisation work together when they need to collaborate, work in teams, and need to connect physically. This is not a new idea, in fact, Charles Handy outlined the 'Shamrock organisation' in his 1991 book *The Age of Unreason*. The Shamrock organisation is made up of an eclectic mix of people, all relevant to the ambition of the organisation or task at hand, and is made up of different levels, capabilities, contracts and working from different locations, all in the quest to solve problems and deliver value.

Although as stated, studies are finding that people are working far more hours than they used to due to the pandemic with shorter commutes and being 'always on' with packed meetings in their schedules, from the start to the end of the day, with no gaps, there is one thing impacting our productivity! The social element of work has disappeared. There is little to no time for simply chatting. The social connection that arguably builds relationships through which things get done is being eroded during this pandemic and this is impacting organisational productivity and performance. Ultimately, it is also harming the well-being of humans. Thus, this will impact work when people formally settle back to post-pandemic ways. If we haven't already, many of us will place a renewed value on the social element of connecting with our employees.

When I worked for a FTSE indexed software company, I remember booking a seat at The Shard, London, where we had an office. This was during the pandemic, when the rules in the UK were more relaxed and people could start to go back in to work under certain conditions. My first day back in the office was quite an experience. It was a warm day and London was empty, so I decided to walk from Tottenham Court Road tube to London Bridge. When I eventually arrived at The Shard, to my amazement, there were only three people in the office, an office that on any other day would have had over a hundred people in it. What really struck me was an interaction I had with one colleague, who was very pleased to see me – we chatted for a while and then with a level of curiosity based on the atmosphere in the office being dead and non-existent, I asked, 'How many times do you come into the office?'

'*Every day,*' was the enthusiastic reply, followed by, 'I miss the interaction!' I initially thought, *what interaction?* Though of course, it was the interaction with people (no matter how few) who come into the office every day. Working from home is not for everyone, but I suspect for an equal number, working from home 'works'. This is a leadership dilemma and will place different demands on leadership going forward, in terms of organising resources for work. Although, as previously stated, we are still not clear as to where we will land, I think many organisations will use the office less and when they do use an office, it will be for collaboration – not to sit and do work in isolation, unless of course you have workers who choose to do that.

The transparency of reality

Back in 2004, one of the biggest power companies in the world commissioned a piece of work designed to answer the question: With the evolving political, technological and societal changes, what will be the expectation of work come 2020? The review team concluded that the generation coming into work (the review surveyed school students and held many focus groups with students across the UK) would need the following:

- **Freedom:** they will want to work in a business culture based on trust and where it is assumed that employees will do their best.
- **EQ:** they will want to work in a business that has a greater awareness of the intuitive and emotional connection needed to effectively lead a business and establish great customer and employee relationships.
- **Meaning:** they will want to work in a business where they are valued and recognised for the work they do and that the work itself has some meaning for them and the wider world.
- **Choice:** they will want to work in a business and do work that meets all their needs, based on the lives they live. They will want to work when, how and where they need to, in order to do what is required.

- **Well-being:** they will want to work in a business that appreciates the whole person at work and provides a work environment that fits with their needs (more on human needs in later chapters).

Rather concerningly, when we fed these findings back to the company's Executive Leadership Team who commissioned the work, the conclusion was that although this generation coming into work will undoubtedly want a different relationship with work, they will not have the ability to change it. The biggest flaw we can see by looking back at 2004 is that society did not foresee the emergence and abundant growth and influence of social platforms, where their voices can now be heard loudly. If we had, I suspect we would have concluded we needed to change the work we offer as a matter of urgency.

There is increasing scrutiny of how businesses and leaders go about their business. How work is experienced, how much people are paid for work and the minimum wages are now known across the globe. Just like you do if you've had a good (or not so good) meal at a restaurant, employees can now leave reviews on social platforms like Glassdoor, which is an American website where employees globally can leave anonymous reviews of companies they work for, as well as view salaries, either when they are working in the company, or when they leave. Glassdoor also provide a CEO rating based on the review of their leadership.

Today, your business brand (i.e., effectively, your reputation, based on what you have done in the past) can be damaged with the slightest of errors, which will negatively impact your reputation in the future. There is a degree of transparency now that *never* existed before and leaders are rightly paying attention.

The social pressure placed on leaders in all walks of life is now at an all-time high, never previously witnessed in the history of work. It was staggering how quickly businesses responded to the death of George Floyd and quickly clarified their position on the situation and racial equality more generally. Silence was viewed as condoning the actions of the police. Recently we have also seen a similar response to the overturning of the Roe v Wade ruling in the US where companies are making sure health care policies support the right of the individual. Businesses are rightly seeing an increase in scrutiny around their Diversity and Inclusion practices and this data will no doubt be a recruitment decision factor for those from ethnic and minority communities, as well as those who no longer want to be just an observer of the inequalities of opportunity across humanity.

The issues and inequalities the world is facing now are front and centre in everyone's world. Today, when we are browsing through our chosen social platforms and news channels from across the globe[5], there are problems that previous generations never knew about, or just simply failed to see. Thanks to social platforms, there is now a pervasive awareness of such issues as:

- 31% of schools still don't have clean water (JMP 2018 Drinking water, sanitation and hygiene in schools, Global baseline report).
- 2 billion people still don't have a decent toilet in their own (WHO/UNICEF Joint Monitoring Programme (JMP) Report 2019).
- 785 million people still don't have clean water close to home (WHO/UNICEF Joint Monitoring Programme (JMP) Report 2019).
- Racial and ethnic discrimination, and other forms of inequality, whether they be local or global.

These issues and others that humanity face need resolving, and increasingly, humans want to join a company that is doing its bit, or at least as a minimum, they are doing no harm. The pressure to resolve these inequalities is being placed less on the governments of the countries concerned but as much, if not more so, on the multinationals that operate within that country. We witnessed this when India was at its worst with the challenges of COVID and there was global pressure placed on pharmaceutical companies to release the patent of their COVID vaccinations and thus, allow the likes of India to create their own answers to quickly and cheaply build COVID immunity. India was a country that manufactured vaccines cheaply for other countries, but for many internal reasons, was unable to help its own people in a time of need by producing its own vaccine. The pharmaceutical sector exists to prolong the life and health of humanity and do good, and yet, at their heart, they are commercial enterprises that also need to profit. Thankfully in this case the global pharmaceuticals placed life before profit.

Globally, there are a growing number of employees looking to right these wrongs by aligning their work to the causes that matter to them. These employees are beginning to choose employment based on whether that potential employer is solving the problems of the world. This is forcing businesses to take a position on things that matter for humanity. We have relied on governments across the world for too long to address regional challenges to humanity, therefore, could now be the time for business *and* government to work together in solving some of the more pressing issues we collectively face?

Whether you work in the public or private sector, we all have an innate need for the relationship we have with work to be a positive one. One where we have a level of pride in the company we donate our time to every day. This is why an employee Net Promoter Score (eNPS) matters, because it measures whether an employee would recommend their employer to another. Moreover, this data provides potential new hires with information on whether current employees are engaged, happy and proud to be working there or not.

> Could the world in which we live be a reflection of how we have created work over the past 150 years?
>
> What if work offered employment *and* the opportunity to solve humanity's problems?

Generational changes in expectations, technological advancements and the inequities that are there for all to see, have resulted in a culture that understandably questions the meaning of work and the value it is bringing to humanity. This level of transparency, along with the age demographic and the huge advances in technology, is creating a seismic shift in the way work will be offered to humanity. This will require us to fundamentally rethink the way we create work and how we lead businesses. Businesses that fail to acknowledge these forces for change now will spend more time being irrelevant than profitable in the future.

The New Purpose of Work

Apart from a level of wealth, humanity has never expressed or demanded more from work up until now. In a world that is now fully connected, humanity needs work to be more than a means of paying your way through life and delivering public services, products, solutions, profit and share value.

I understand why people say the purpose of work is to make money. I get it! But that is no longer enough. Look at the news for a day and you clearly see the way COVID has ravaged some parts of the world due to poor leadership and/or insubstantial infrastructure. I believe this is teaching humanity a valuable lesson. When the next pandemic comes (and it will), we need a world that has greater levels of leadership that has built substantial infrastructure to be able to overcome those times. When humanity faces its next threat, if we do not all have access to rudimentary resources like clean air, water and basic medical equipment, then this COVID period will be a stain on humanity's history and its ability to learn and adapt. We must question and evolve work to resolve these challenges the best we can, and we can only do that if we openly learn and adapt from what learning recent years offer us and begin to question the purpose of work.

Humanity needs a different relationship with work and the nature of work itself needs to change if we are to see and experience a different reality. Whether in the public or private sector, organisations across the globe need to be of value to humanity – this will be the key to organisational success in the future.

It's not like businesses have not seen this coming – 'how to do better' has been on the business agenda for quite some time, but I think the business world and its investors have been viewing the idea as too utopian and placed it in the 'soft, pink and fluffy' box.

As a result of this pandemic and other factors we have outlined, more businesses are needing to step up and grapple with this idea that the purpose of work is ultimately for the good of humanity, and I say that because some leaders and businesses (not all) have seemingly partnered with COVID and harmed society.

> Problems bring out the best in humanity, much more than targets, profit and share value.

In times of change it will be those businesses willing to learn and adapt that will stay relevant and profitable. The problems we are facing now are making us question the purpose of work and, over the coming chapters, we will go into more detail on how, as a leader you can create exceptional work *and* be of service to humanity.

The factors we have outlined in this chapter are influencing a change in the way humanity experiences work. I propose that the purpose of work in the future will be to do three things *extraordinarily* well:

1. **Do Great** – to be a place of work that overcomes, collaborates, thrives and succeeds.
2. **Do Good** – to be a place of work that positively impacts society.
3. **Be Well** – to be a place of work that nourishes humanity.

Work's purpose has always been to do great. Let's face it, if you are not great at what you do, then certainly in the private sector, you're unlikely to be in business. What humanity has never explicitly expressed as a need of business is to do good *and* be well.

Well-designed and executed work enhances the lives it touches with the services, products and solutions it creates, as well as the communities and societies it works within.

Businesses that have these three purposes of work implicitly entwined into their strategy will naturally become iconic businesses. These organisations will attract the best talent and readily be able to create and develop their own talent internally. Over time these organisations will also attract more investor interest and support.

There is a natural 'virtuous circle' here that creates a competitive advantage when all three purposes of work become reality. When organisations create great places of work, where the human thrives *and* does good, it creates a place of work that has energy, passion and focus. This requires a different level of leadership – leadership that more than ever before meets the vital human needs for meaning, growth, belonging and attention – more on these later.

There are a growing number of businesses that have the three purposes of work integrated into their strategies and I predict there will be more in the future. I hope I'm wrong, but I also predict it will be a slow evolution of work towards a point in time where all businesses build in the three purposes to the way they operate. The reason it will be slow is twofold; firstly, as we face more humanitarian challenges over the next few decades, more governments will start to see businesses as allies in addressing and overcoming the challenges in the way they tax and incentivise businesses to operate from their countries; and secondly, the investment sector has yet to fully align to backing and supporting those businesses that not only do great, but also do good and are places of work where the human thrives.

This is the leadership challenge for the 21st century. In this chapter, we have covered the current state of work and what needs to change to make the purpose of work more aligned to the needs of humanity. Now, let's hold an honest review of the current state of leadership globally.

Chapter Two: Fish rot from the head down

The chapter heading probably gives you a sense of where we are going on leadership, so let's start by stating the world needs a cadre of leaders who are fit for the 21st century. Humanity is in dire need of leaders who are not just able to build great businesses, but also contribute to a better world for generations to come. Like many of you, I have listened to story after story of irresponsible, self-centred, duplicitous and quite frankly, dangerous leadership that all so often brings business institutions, public services and countries to their knees.

The business schools and establishments that have shaped and developed leadership now need to ask whether their curriculum is fit for today's world, and I say this as a person who has spent the last 20 plus years developing leaders: leaders who are unable to build profitable and sustainable businesses that are good places to work, and that do good in the world, should not be in control of their own TV set, let alone a business.

Leadership is an expectation. It is an expectation of a better future. It is not manifested in a particular role, level, or a hierarchy; rather, it is a set of innate capabilities that bring the best out of humans for the good of humanity. To be a leader at any level, in any context, is to recognise that you have influence to create a better future.

Leadership is a capability, not a role

I stated in the previous chapter that you are a leader if the welfare of others is core to who you are and what you do. Yes, leadership can be nurtured, developed and to a degree, taught, but it cannot be assumed by simply an appointment. If you ever wanted a lesson in whether leaders are born or developed, just switch on the TV and listen to your local news channels. Your news will be littered with people who, because of fate, or sheer hard work, find themselves in a position that requires leadership and go on to do extraordinary things to better humanity. These people have 'laws' named after them, named in honour of the people they fought to right a wrong for. The world is full of stories of mums who have lost their sons to careless drivers, who lead successful campaigns for greater speed restrictions in their local area, or dads who had lost their daughters to drugs, who go on to lead a successful campaign to increase local policing. What do all these leaders have in common? A need to make things better and a desire to commit to action. They weren't born leaders; they took up the role and became one, which means all of us can be leaders if we have an inner cause worth fighting for, or a role that demands and expects the best from us.

If you are making things worse for humanity, the chances are you are more likely to be a narcissistic, egocentric, despot, dictator, whose only needs worth meeting are your own.

On a grand scale, weak, narcissistic and incompetent leadership can cause untold misery to millions. As we have found with the COVID pandemic, it can also cost lives. This standard of leadership on the political stage, as well as the myopic rationale leaders hold for simply profit at all costs in business, must change if, we as a species, are to stand any chance of continuing to inhabit the world in which we live. We need leaders who do better than their predecessors.

The leadership shadow

Globally, over the past 20 years, we have witnessed shameful failings of leadership. News outlets have been littered with articles detailing the decline and 'erosion' in 'trust' in leaders in all walks of life; from the church, to politics, to commerce. Over the past 10 years, globally there has been a litany of companies in the public and private sector that have displayed little regard for rules and legislation, and leaders who have been less than truthful or prudent in their choices, let alone their moral leadership and in doing so, have broken humanity's trust.

Alone the following examples demonstrate poor leadership, collectively they question the very health of leadership in today's world.

Privatising the UK Rail Network

After the privatisation of the UK Rail industry in 1995, from 1995 to 2008, a total of 82 people were killed and over 1,318 injured on UK rail networks. It was a disgraceful example of leadership and the myopic drive for profit.[6]

The reality was that, rather than humans inspecting the train tracks, poor equipment and technology were used in a culture that bred apathy. With the Paddington crash that happened in October 1999, killing 31 and injuring 523, the coroner summed up the findings and stated, 'There was a serious and persistent failure to convene signal sighting committees as they should have been, because of the changes to the signals and the fact that signals had been repeatedly passed at danger. This was due to a combination of incompetent management and inadequate procedures.'

The privatised companies stated that when they picked up the running of the rail networks from the Government in 1995, the tracks were in a poor state of repair and yet, they knowingly continued services. It was only after the spate of headline crashes that they were forced by the UK Government to invest in rail network infrastructure.

What drives leaders of a private enterprise to knowingly run a dangerous and under-invested rail service? My contention is that this comes about because of two factors; firstly, a narrow obsession with goals, objectives, financial targets and profit at the expense of all other factors (often driven by bonus and incentive plans); and secondly, organisational dissonance, i.e., when an organisation can say one thing and be another, without it seemingly causing an issue. Common examples of this are organisations that state they 'value their people' and yet they exploit child labour in third world countries, or in the case of the rail industry, are heavily focussed on 'profit and shareholder value', whilst 'neglecting the safety of the very people who use their train tracks'.

Healthcare leadership cares, right?

You would expect leaders in healthcare to have one thing and one thing only on their mind: the care, safety and effective treatment of the patients in their care, but sadly, this isn't always true. It is widely believed that outsourcing NHS cleaning in the late 90s, with the aim of bringing better value to public spending, was greatly responsible for the MRSA bug that, at its height in 2003/04, killed approximately 6000 people in the UK. The UK didn't have MRSA on this scale in the mid-90s! A change in Government and more autonomy for local healthcare leaders in the UK, along with tighter targets on funding, was a perfect storm that led to the MRSA outbreak.

Unintended consequences

It turns out that increasing overall exam results by expelling students who have low grade projections has unintended consequences. Permanent school exclusions in England have been rising since 2013. In a letter dated 2019 from the then Major of London, Sadiq Khan, to police commissioners, he wrote:

'We firmly believe it is unacceptable that young people

can be ejected from the formal education process in this way, when we know how vulnerable they become to being sucked into criminality as a result... Our schools are facing significant funding pressures and many interventions for our most vulnerable children are being cut. This cannot be right and schools must have the necessary resources to deliver good interventions and support to those at risk of exclusion.'

The letter highlighted that in two of the country's knife crime hot spots, London and the West Midlands, permanent exclusions had risen by 62% and 40% respectively since 2013-14. It added: 'Clearly, the way the education system deals with excluded young people is broken... It cannot be right that so many of those who have committed offences have been excluded from school or were outside of mainstream education.' By excluding those students unwilling to learn and in doing so, increasing the school's average exam grades, school leaders inadvertently increased knife crime.

A drop in the ocean

In April 2010, BP's leadership failure to adhere to the correct levels of maintenance and safety procedures, which led to the infamous 'Deepwater Horizon' disaster, the biggest recorded marine oil spill in the history of the industry, with untold damage to nature and human livelihood. The legal penalties cost $20BN (and are still rising).

More broadly, across the globe, there have been equally concerning leadership failings.

There to help

In 2011, senior OXFAM officials were 'allowed' to resign after an internal investigation found that they had hired sex workers for orgies. The charity should have been in Haiti relieving the country's devastation after the 2010 earthquake that killed thousands, not exploiting its misery.

Conflict of interest

In May 2012, Sketchers' claims that their toning shoe helped tone muscle and led to calorie loss when consumers walked in them were found to be false when it was uncovered that one such research study commissioned by Sketchers was carried out by a chiropractor who was married to a Sketcher's marketing executive. The legal penalty was $40M.

What is in this?

In 2013, Findus products claiming to be beef products were in fact found to contain traces of horse meat. Some products were found to contain 100% horse meat and in 23 out of 27 beef burgers, there were traces of pig DNA. The legal penalty cost was $100m+.

A basic need

In the middle of a 2014 US drought, Nestle bought 50 million gallons of water from Sacramento and sold it back to residents at 1000% profit, with the Nestle Chairman even asserting that 'water was not a basic right'. The legal penalty was $32bn (which, incidentally, is how much Nestle made from selling bottled water).

Fuming

In 2015, 'Dieselgate' started when Volkswagen were found guilty by the US Environmental Protection Agency (EPA) because they fitted what were known as 'defeat devices' to their diesel cars, which included software that would detect when the cars were undergoing laboratory testing and turn on controls to reduce nitrogen emissions. The cars would then appear to comply with the agency's standards but, in some cases, were actually emitting up to 40 times the nitrogen dioxide limit when on the road.

Remote control

In 2017, 'Batterygate' hit Apple when a Reddit user reported that a software update had reduced the performance of their iPhone, but that this had corrected itself when they replaced the battery. This led to a lot of press coverage, where some reporters accused Apple of forcing users to upgrade their iPhone by deliberately slowing devices as they aged. Tim Cook (CEO of Apple at the time) issued a statement on the matter a week after the news broke, confirming that the software was designed to throttle performance, but claiming that the intent was only to prevent unexpected shutdowns, which could affect devices with older batteries. The company offered a discount on battery replacements as a gesture of goodwill for those affected.

Misuse of data

In March 2018, a big scandal hit Facebook (now Meta), when *The New York Times* and the *Guardian* reported that a firm called Global Science Research had harvested data from 87 million Facebook users in 2013 without explicit consent. The data was then passed on to Cambridge Analytica, where it was used to create highly targeted and sophisticated political campaigns to vote for Trump and Brexit, and in doing so, threatening the very democracy many of us have the privilege to live under.

Unfulfillment

There have been numerous articles written about how poorly Amazon treat their staff, to the point where some employees in the US are looking to join the Retail, Wholesale and Department Store Union (RWDSU) to protect employee rights and establish more fitting work standards.

And finally

Who in the UK from a private sector perspective can ever forget the sad case of Baby 'P', who died from continual abuse that had gone unnoticed by social care workers from Haringey Council? After an interview between the BBC's John Humphrys and the Haringey Council representative, the council leader concluded by stating that the council had 'followed procedures'. John retorted, 'Yes, but at the end of this "perfect" paper trail is a dead baby'.

I considered whether it was right to put in this last example because UK councils are under huge pressure with minimal resource to do things right all the time, an almost impossible task. The reason I left the example in was that when I heard the interview, I was struck by the leader of the council's view that it was the procedure that failed Baby P, not the council. In all these examples, it would be easy for leaders to blame and excuse their failings on internal processes, failing to recognise the fact that they as leaders need to take accountability for what is happening under their leadership.

What does this all mean?

It's very easy to read these examples, along with many others on a daily basis, and view them as organisational failings, but the truth is that somewhere, someone did something that created the conditions that either led to the indiscretion or failing, or directly caused the problem. Leadership and the lack of it is at the heart of every one of these failings and all the others we, as humanity, face. Organisations and institutions don't make mistakes or become racist, belligerent and hostile places of work;

people do. These leaders had the welfare of others as part of their role and they failed. The future will be a cruel teacher if we do not learn and adapt our leadership to what these, and numerous other examples, are telling us about the state of our leadership across the political, public, and private sector.

Although these examples are in many ways extreme, what drives this standard of leadership is its uncompromisingly myopic focus on the outcomes (i.e., profit, revenue, positive reputation, too efficient service levels etc.), rather than taking into account the wider human and community impact of their choices. I challenge you again to listen to your local news and daily you will hear numerous stories, wherever you are in the world, of leadership failings that don't make major headlines, but nonetheless, negatively impact humanity. Failings, that had the leader placed the welfare of others first (our universal human needs), the issue or failing would potentially not have occurred.

For many notable brands, there has been a void of morality and ethics in big business. As the old saying goes, 'it only takes one bad apple to spoil the bunch'. That said, one notable change to the scandals that have hit business over recent years is that they have become more severe from humanity's perspective. Not only do they question the moral validity of the leadership within these companies, but they also question the validity and truthfulness of the data that shapes the world, and this allows people to question the whole foundation on which the world operates. 'Fake news' isn't new; it has been around since the birth of the Roman Empire, but in a world where there is more connectivity, transparency and influence through media channels, we *must* define and demand a higher standard of leadership, otherwise everything that underpins our societies will be drawn into question. Whether it is the manipulation of data to swing votes, the development of software to influence buying habits, or as stated previously the numerous big companies that have been skipping around the world on various 'tax evasion' tours, we need a different level of ethical and moral leadership. The world is facing a different phase in its evolution and if we are not careful, the leadership that underpins the global economy (and other institutions) will fracture the pillars on which society functions. Integrity is as much a characteristic as a skill, and we all have it. It is about doing the right thing. It is about doing what you say you are going to do. It is about total alignment between what you feel, think, say and do and it will be what humanity is drawn to in the future. The problem now is that leaders are forced to question and override their integrity every day by making decisions that favour profit or popularity, over what's right for the human.

People trust people, *not* organisations, institutions, or establishments; we must create leadership that increases trust

In all my research on leadership there are few better examples of a leader with integrity than Mahatma Gandhi and the way he conducted his visit to England in 1931. At the height of the British Raj's power in India, Gandhi was renowned as a voice of dissent. Churchill once described him as a 'a seditious Middle Temple lawyer, now posing as a fakir of a type well known in the East, striding half-naked up the steps of the Viceregal palace'. But Gandhi was nothing less than persistent in his aim of bringing the British Raj to its knees. To further his aim, in 1931, he decided to visit Great Britain (September to December) to convince the British of the unfairness the Raj was exerting over India. On his visit, Gandhi made a point of going to Lancashire. The aim of the visit was to highlight the fact that Britain's exports of yarn and cloth to India were causing high levels of unemployment in his own country. He wanted to encourage the millworkers to see his side of the argument in the debate over the unemployment caused by his boycott.

As he explained to the workers: 'You have three million unemployed, but we have nearly three hundred million unemployed. Your average unemployment dole is seventy shillings a month. Our average income is seven shillings and sixpence a month.' It is widely accepted that his visit did not achieve its ultimate aims, however the spectacle of Gandhi in loincloth and sandals with bare legs made a favourable impression with the British public. How Gandhi did this was revealed in an interaction with the British press after he had delivered an address to the House of Commons, the seat of the British Government. In an over two-hour address, he never stumbled over his words; he spoke clearly, compellingly and without a break about his cause for a free India, independent of British rule. When he finished, he was given a round of applause by a packed House. After the address, Gandhi's Press Officer was questioned by the British press. The questions were along the lines of, 'How did Gandhi manage to pull that off?' 'How long did it take him to memorize the speech?' Gandhi's Press Officer was perplexed and was not able to answer the questions, until eventually he responded with, 'What you don't seem to understand is that what he (Gandhi) feels, he thinks, what he thinks, he says and what is he says, he does'. In other words, 'he' *was* the message.

This level of leadership integrity is hard to come by, but that should not stop us from seeking out ways in which we can help leaders uncover it, develop it and live it, and so ensure these leaders find positions of influence and leadership in the right organisations. Jim Collins, in his book *Good to Great (2001)* [7], identified what he termed 'Level 5' leadership, and went on to describe this level of leadership as leaders who are a powerful mixture of personal humility and indomitable will. They're incredibly ambitious, but their ambition is, first and foremost, for the cause, for the organisation and its purpose, not themselves. This links meaning (the cause) and trust (the relationship) with what leadership needs to be to create an iconic company

Trust (and the lack of it) has not been helped by the wider lack of ethical and moral leadership in other institutions, be that in governments and religious institutions, around the world. Like any relationship, if you cannot trust 'the other', there is an awful lot of energy expended in keeping up the right level of appearance. It is my observation that many (not so iconic) organisations place a lot of focus on creating systems, controls and processes and put them in place to make sure people do the right thing. I am referring to more traditional practices like management by objective (MBO) values and behaviours, performance management, time and attendance, governance and policies etc. Why, after hiring the person, do we not trust that the person will deliver? On the one hand, when we offer the role, we are saying, 'Great, you are exactly what we are looking for', and then as soon as they are in the role, we are myopically focused on whether they will deliver.

Learning is key

Organisations don't make mistakes, *people* do. All too often leaders, whether in the political or commercial space, have been trained to communicate *all which is good* and so continue the positive propaganda, whilst ignoring the need to answer and own up to that which was wrong.[8] They think they get away with it by not admitting they were wrong, when in fact, what they have traded is a positive message that in return erodes trust. The problem with this position is that it isolates the leader because everyone knows what should have been said, but now, no one says it for fear of being contrary to what the leader has communicated. This starts to isolate the leader and an isolated leader quickly becomes out of touch, out of date and out of service. History is littered with them. Out of the public eye, a leader can ask, 'What could have been done better?' But in the public eye, building trust should be the priority, hence 'owning' the failing. Leaders need to be able to own their mistakes, not defend them, so that learning can take place and, just as importantly, public trust can be restored. I understand there are legal issues at play here, but surely, we should be encouraging a level of openness and I say that because to recognise and own one's mistake is the foundation on which we, as humans, learn. Rather than the media asking a leader bluntly: 'Can you admit a mistake was made?' perhaps a more useful question for the sake of humanity would be, 'What would you do differently in the future to change the outcome?' This question presumes a level of failure, and in answering, the leader admits that things could have been different and is able to articulate what will be better going forward, and so builds trust, hope and optimism in their answer. I don't think I am alone when I say I'd rather see leaders encounter that level of journalism rather than the pointless, 'Tell us you messed up and you're an idiot' type of questioning that often goes on and serves the public broadcasts with sensational TV and increases the popularity of the interviewer rather than the interviewee.

Light in the darkness

You're probably thinking at this point that I have majored on the negative in relation to the work and leadership front and you'd be right. I have wondered whether it is too much, but I am sad that we have got to a place in history where we accept that businesses are corrupt, and leaders are not to be trusted. We should expect more and on a more positive COVID front, we have seen some excellent examples of leadership when humanity has been at the forefront of its focus. In a *Forbes* article ('What Do Countries With The Best Coronavirus Responses Have In Common? Women Leaders'[9],) Avivah Wittenberg-Cox made the case that countries where women leaders led had lower counts of COVID infection and deaths – why was this? The article cites the female leaders from Germany, Taiwan, New Zealand, Iceland, Finland, Norway and Denmark as being decisive and yet empathetic in winning over their nations' response to dealing with the pandemic. These leaders immediately took the outbreak seriously. Avivah goes on to cite the case that, 'among the first and the fastest responses was from Tsai Ing-wen in Taiwan. Back in January 2020, at the first sign of a new illness, she introduced 124 measures to block the spread without having to resort to the lockdowns that have become common elsewhere. She is now sending 10 million face masks to the U.S. and Europe. Tsai managed what CNN has called "among the world's best" responses, keeping the epidemic under control, still reporting only six deaths.' Avivah also cites the case of Norway's Prime Minister, Erna Solberg, who had the innovative idea of using television to talk directly to her country's children. She was building on the short, 3-minute press conference that Danish Prime Minister Mette Frederiksen had held a couple of days earlier. Solberg held a dedicated press conference where no adults were allowed. She responded to kids' questions from across the country, taking time to explain why it was OK to feel scared. The originality of the idea takes one's breath away. How many other simple, humanity-led innovations would more female leadership unleash?

Dealing with dilemmas

The business of leadership is to deal with dilemmas. Leaders must wrestle daily with paradoxes: global v. local, compete v. collaborate, change v. maintain, short v. long-term, internal v. external, past v. future, known v. unknown, action v. reflection, numbers v. people, etc. In the case of COVID, the political leadership dilemma was economy v. health. If you had to choose a leader who made decisions on the likely impact on the economy due to this pandemic, or one that made decisions on the human cost of this pandemic – which would you choose? I suspect you would place humanity first in this instance, and yet, it is neither one or the other; human-centred leadership in this instance is about dealing with the economy *and* the health of humanity. The reality is that some leaders globally have clearly placed a higher focus on one to the detriment of the other because it is a leadership dilemma few have ever had to face before.

When the world is in crisis, we need leadership that is clear, confident and caring in its approach and is able to hold conflicting points of view in their mind and effectively wrestle with them both. **Clear** because people want clarity on what is happening and the impact it is having. **Confident** because people want to trust their leaders to be honest and to do the right thing. **Caring** because leaders who listen and gain a greater sense of what is *really* going on, will more likely make better decisions. As this pandemic draws to a close, it will no doubt reveal some telling insights into the impact global leadership has had on humanity.

> F. Scott Fitzgerald's quote on intelligence could be easily applied to that of leadership: 'The test of a first-rate intelligence is the ability to hold two opposing ideas in mind at the same time and still retain the ability to function'.

Before we go any further, I just want to say that I have a lot of respect and admiration for leaders in today's world. It is not easy, I know because I am one and I work with many. Across all sectors, I have come across leaders who have inspired me and made me a better leader and person as a result. Many leaders I have come across over the years have been highly intelligent, thoughtful, driven and compassionate people and have inspired others to overcome seemingly impossible challenges. They have had to make difficult decisions, many of which negatively impact the employees that work for them, and yet these are decisions that keep the business alive for the employees that are left. Many organisations view leadership as a differentiator in their organisational performance and rightly invest heavily in ensuring the right leaders have the capabilities needed to lead their business. Mistakes will always be made in business and as a result, leaders must continually learn and adapt to the challenges they face, and we must do all we can to help them do so.

The only constant in leadership is incompetence.

Yesterday – Today - Tomorrow

For us to anticipate and propose leadership that is relevant for tomorrow, we must firstly look at where leadership has come from, where it is now and where it needs to go in the future.

In 1712, Thomas Newcomen built the first successful steam engine, and it was steam that was really the lifeblood of the industrial revolution. The industrial revolution saw the birth of factories, mills and subsequently, people moved from farming fields into towns to help lend their labour to the industrial revolution, where the focus was on making things. The focus of leaders in these early days was on how efficiently both machines and people could operate and drive production.

Roll on to the early 20th century and Frederick Taylor was the first to investigate and analyse the efficiency of industry and the impact on management. He looked at management through the lens of science. Taylor believed in 'a fair day's pay for a fair day's work' and that people were intrinsically motivated by money. It was this motivation that drove productivity and if a worker did not achieve enough in a day, then he didn't deserve to be paid as much as another worker who was more productive.

As industry's needs grew, production was key. When the knowledge economy came along in the 1950s, it was all about data and a human's comprehension of what could be improved. The initial foundation for the knowledge economy [10] was introduced in 1967 in the book *The Effective Executive* by Peter Drucker. In the book, Drucker states that the personal capital of knowledge workers is 'knowledge', and many knowledge worker jobs require a lot of thinking and manipulating information, as opposed to moving or crafting physical objects. Then came computers!

With the advent of computer technology, all the manipulation began to be computerised and the need for human comprehension of data began to decline. A great example of this was Walmart and their use of technology when they pushed for the barcode to become the standard way of identifying products. The Universal Product Code (UPC) was approved in 1973. As former Walmart store leader, Jon Lehman, explained[11], through the bar code, Walmart was able to 'track sales on specific items, specific weeks, specific days, specific hours of the day, when [they] sell merchandise the most.' Through this knowledge, the company has managed to change its relationship with manufacturers and suppliers. It has, according to Lehman, 'completely changed the communication process between Walmart and its manufacturers … It took Walmart from an archaic, old-build way of communicating with a vendor once a week, to communicating every day, every hour, every minute'. This is a relevant example of how, in the knowledge economy, computer technology shifted the management focus from simple data to useful and valuable information.

The challenge facing leaders today is how to create teams and organisations that can interpret valid data quickly and so make informed decisions for their business or use it to gain competitive advantage at pace.

Leading today is *very different* than what it was even 20 years ago. The pace at which leaders work today and the amount of data most leaders need to digest and understand, along with our insatiable appetite for 'speed' and 'more', is creating organisational cultures that simply rely on a bias for action. We have less time to think and make sense of what is going on in highly complex organisational structures so the only thing we tend to value is activity. The result is that many organisations are places where people are busy being unintentionally useless, and in many cases, burning themselves out as part of the process. The worst performing organisations are those that place an emphasis and value on activity with little consideration on impact. The unfortunate aspect to this current situation is that most, if not all, organisations possess the resources and intelligence to overcome most of their challenges, they simply do not have the time, or place the value on taking the time to fully understand the problems they face so they can collectively overcome their challenges. Leaders must be able to view their impact and when the impact needs course correction, have the humility and intelligence to make the right next decision.

Organisational Health

It is the role of the leader to access and unleash the potential of the organisation and to do it in a way that does not damage the human spirit. The inconvenient truth is that due to the pace of change, increased competition, the deluge of data, 'more for less', higher levels of activity and a tighter reliance on management by data, many organisations should have a health warning attached to them. Placing total energy and resources on achievement of targets, a value on activity rather than impact, and little to no regard for the care of their workforce - many organisations are sick and this is making its employees unwell as a result. There seems to be little regard or indeed science behind reducing headcount in organisations today. Usually a percentage figure is given as a target that aligns to a cost or saving. Sizing the job role and working on the basis of reducing activity if you take people out of the business seems to be a forgotten art. Remove heads and their activity is picked up by their employees – job done. It seems odd that if you go to a restaurant and you are fed food that has been made by people not adhering to clean work practices and you report that they made you sick; in most countries, that would be looked into for fear of those practices making others unwell or sick, and yet everyday thousands of people go to work in places that harm them physically or mentally through poor working practices and leadership and nothing is done about it.

Although in the UK, the amount of sick days have maintained a certain level since 2010, the reasons for sickness have changed. Over the years, the common reason for sickness – a cold or flu – has been replaced with stress, depression or anxiety and musculoskeletal disorders, which now account for the majority of days lost due to work-related ill health[12]. Now, of course this could be attributed to many things: the societal strains of everyday life, more openness to report such issues, personal pressure and increasing fatigue and stress. I, however, think leadership has a bearing on this too.

An article in *Daily Mail* stated[13] that sickness levels in industry are estimated to cost the UK economy more than £13 billion a year, with nearly one in eight days off sick thought to be a feigned illness. How do they know this? They saw a pattern emerge between more sick days on a Friday and Monday either before or after public holidays. The paper went on to outline a solution to this problem and it was this: we have the technology to use Voice Risk Analysis (VRA) systems (lie detection technology to you and me) on phone lines now so that when the employee calls in to report his or her sickness, the VRA system will tell their leader whether they are lying or actually sick by picking up the changes in a caller's voice. It didn't go on to say whether VRA would be able to differentiate between physically sick or mentally sick for work, but in my view, I have come across far too many who are 'mentally' sick and tired of work. Rather than question the trust of your employees by finding out who is lying and who isn't, wouldn't it be more useful to ask 'why' more humans are becoming sick and tired of work? Thankfully this technology didn't take off, although many organisations since the 80s in the UK have been applying the Bradford Factor as a way of weighting unplanned absences, supporting the principle that repeat absences have a greater operational impact than longer-term sickness. Using the Bradford calculator, those who take shorter yet more frequent time off sick, score higher than those who take longer less frequent time off. As a result, I have heard that some people have been told that if they are going to 'pull a sicky' don't do the odd day, *do a week*! From a leadership perspective, surely it is better to understand the reasons for time off and understand what you can do as a leader to mitigate time away from work?

In the US, one-third of Americans[14] are living with extreme stress and nearly half of Americans (48%) believe that their stress has increased over the past five years. Stress is taking a toll on people — contributing to health problems, poor relationships and lost productivity at work, according to a new national survey released by the American Psychological Association (APA).

In many other countries, the poor health of people due to working conditions is causing a huge burden on healthcare resources.

Of course, when you impart statistics such as these, there are many factors to take into consideration, with the impact of work being one of them. I share these statistics because I believe it is the responsibility of leadership to bring some level of relief from stress when humans come to work. Why is it that when research tells us that humans do not function and perform well under *continual* levels of stress, we continue to place considerable pressures and stress into the system of work, and all too often ask employees to pick up the impossible job?

I remember being at a seminar with 500 HR leaders and Ricardo Semler was speaking about employee engagement. Ricardo was known for being a maverick in his approach and challenged the HR leaders in the room to validate why so many senior HR leaders spend millions of pounds on consultants to find out how motivated and optimistic their staff are through engagement surveys, when he said there is only one question you need to ask. At this point, I sadly report that you could loudly hear the rustle for pens and notepads from my peers as we eagerly grabbed something with which to capture this soon-to-arrive piece of brilliance. Then a silence descended as everyone was poised, pen in hand, for his next sentence. 'The question you need to ask is, what do I need to do to get you into work and for you to do your best *every day*?' On that note, the whole audience gave an exasperated breath of '*Is that it*?' Ricardo seemingly failed to deliver in that moment, but was that really the case? Might there, within that bland punchline, lie an exceptional insight? I think so. It's not rocket science, really it isn't, although maybe if we pay millions for it, we value it more, but really if leaders asked the people they led 'What do I need to do to get you into work and for you to do your best every day?' – what would be the impact? I suspect it may increase organisational health and overall engagement, productivity and performance and *not* burn people out.

Organisational health is a necessary precursor to sustained high performance. With the levels of transparency we have in today's world, we are but a click away from finding out which leaders are toxic to work for and which leaders are not.

Leadership needs to be better

Today, we have an opportunity to rethink leadership. The world has been changing radically in the last 40 years and leaders have struggled to keep up. One of the most popular dilemmas organisations face today is to 'predict the future skills they need going forward'. The truth is that we couldn't predict the future in the past and we're not able to predict the future in the present, all we can do is adapt to and 'shape' the future now. Yes, we have 'tweaked' the leadership role to move away from being directive and hierarchical to a more levelled, influential, collaborative and empowering style (who can remember 'leader as coach'?), and yet a leader's role is still essentially the same today as it was a hundred years ago, i.e., the management of human capital for the commercial benefit of business.

Over the years I have worked for, and with, some exceptional leaders, who were able to lead short-term objectives with long-terms aims. These leaders were able to engage and energise their 'flock' at times of need, and even when it was bad news, were able to impart the news is a way that people understood and accepted. When Winston Churchill said that, 'tact was the ability to tell someone to go to hell in such a way that they look forward to the trip', he could easily have been describing leadership. These leaders were also able to relate to others and be humble enough to listen, and so at times, when it is right to do so, be 'led by others. When no one else wanted to step forward, they become the ones who stepped into the breach. These leaders have successful work lives, as well as personal lives, and have a strong yearning to succeed in both domains and have the awareness and fortitude to bring magic to both. For these leaders, it is also not about how much money they have accumulated, but their drivers are more directed to the impact their leadership is having on the people close to them and the world around them. This is the leadership we need to recognise, value and develop.

From any field of leadership, if I was to ask you who in history you would cast as a Saint or a Sinner, I suspect you would have no issues with compiling a list from either camp because their legacy is left for all to see. Depending on your political view, you could argue the toss on some of the characters that have come to the fore in recent times. In the UK, leaders like Thatcher, Churchill and Blair all continue to divide opinion, as do Trump, Clinton, Obama and Biden in the US; however, in the business world, if I was to ask you to write a similar list based on whether they are a Saint or a Sinner, I suspect you may find this a more difficult task. Unless leaders fit into the shoes of Indra Nooyi, Bill Gates, Sheryl Sandberg, Satya Nadella, Carly Fiorina, Elon Musk, Jeff Bezos, Jack Dorsey, Marc Benioff, Daniel Ek or Richard Branson, most others are unknown to a great majority of us. That said, these leaders and the impact that their peers have on us as humanity is huge, and we should never underestimate this impact, which is not only based on the products, solutions and services these leaders provide, but also the way they treat their employees and the influence they have in the world in which we live. At a personal level, these leaders can make or break your day. They can help make your dreams come true or destroy them.

In an article in the UK *Times*[15], Chuka Umunna called for a change in the way we look at business. He made a valid point when he asked, rather than looking at business as either 'good' or 'bad', we should instead ask, 'What characteristics add value to a company and to our economy at the same time and what can be done to nurture them?'

It's a great question. What does add value? We proposed in the previous chapter that the value of a business should come from doing **great**, doing **good** and being a place where humans do **well**.

What if the Hippocratic oath was applied not just to physicians but also to leaders in the political, public and private sectors? The Hippocratic oath states, 'I will follow that system of regimen which, according to my ability and judgment, I consider for the benefit of my patients [the people I serve, i.e., employees and customers], and abstain from whatever is deleterious and mischievous.' You could argue that this is of course slightly facetious, but where is the global standard by which we hold leaders to account and should there, in today's world, be one?

We should look at leadership as a set of capabilities *and* attributes and professionalise them accordingly. Business schools should adjust curricula to meet the needs of 'human-centred work' design, where the leadership focus is on creating work that advances society. A leader's purpose is to create a place of work that harnesses and unleashes human potential for the benefit of society, such that it becomes successful.

Fish rot from the head down and so do institutions and organisations.

So far, we have looked at work and leadership and made the case for change based on its impact on humanity. At this point you would be forgiven in thinking that so far, the picture painted is one of duplicity, darkness and despair, but all the indications are that things are looking up. Leaders are starting to consider the possibility of placing humanity at the centre of their endeavours and it is beginning to pay dividends.

But who are these leaders and how are they taking a more humanistic view?

Over the following chapters we will explore four fundamental human needs that not only unleash our potential to excel, they also create a place of work where business prospers. In the final chapter, I will propose a Leadership Manifesto to summarise the human need of work and leadership going forward and invite you to post your leadership oath and share your stories of when leadership has lifted you and brought out the best in you.

Chapter Three: Meaning instead of hopelessness

What is the business of your business? Who does your business really serve? Why should people get out of bed and come to work for you every day? All these questions and the answers to them create meaning for the people who work and support your endeavour.

As humans, we are 'meaning-making' machines. Life without meaning breeds hopelessness, which is becoming ever more pervasive in society today. Meaning gave us all a reason to get out of bed this morning and I suggest how quickly you got out of bed is down to the level of meaning you have in your life. Meaning is fundamental to our lives. It is the source of our energy, purpose, focus and passion. Find your meaning and it is like filling up your energy tank with fuel every day; lose your meaning and your energy tank becomes empty, and when it is empty, you find it difficult to be interested in anyone or anything. It feels like you are wearing a 'coat of fog', heavy and blinding. Life becomes a never-ending drudgery of nothingness. In extreme cases, this becomes the start of depression, an increasing diagnosis for humanity.

Meaning matters

In the previous chapter, on the state of leadership, we listed some of the more known infamous 'leadership indiscretions' that have happened over the past 20 plus years at a global level, sometimes with tragic consequences for humanity. These 'indiscretions' are evident in business, as well as other institutions, such as politics and religion, and many (if not all) leaders in those institutions have a responsibility to uphold moral and ethical standards. Sadly, some leaders in politics and religion have been found wanting in their moral and ethical standards. If this continues, it will undoubtedly lead to humanity questioning their very own beliefs and faith in leadership and this will be terribly destabilising. In a vacuum of meaning, anything or anyone could come to the fore. Any belief system could be replaced. As humans, either we will search for and feel the void with a belief system that is right for us and so create meaning, or we will follow one that maybe isn't.

> Leadership must build meaning to create a wider value for humanity.

From a societal point of view, all the indicators point towards us, as humans, lacking meaning more now than ever before. We seem to be spending our time in distraction mode, glued to our devices, searching aimlessly across social media platforms and media boxsets for something of either interest or just plain distraction. There is far too much distraction today, which is causing a disengagement with real life. Our brain seems to be searching, like a radio scanning the airwaves for the next clear channel, hoping that it speaks to us in some way and so becomes a 'calling' of sorts. What time we don't use aimlessly searching for meaning is then filled with either sleep or work.

Firstly, you would have to ask what is the meaning of work and then what does humanity derive from it? Of course, the simple and commonly 'trotted out' response to these two questions is that the purpose of work is to provide a service, solution or product that makes a profit and, secondly, humans come to work to make money, which provides financial security of sorts. For most businesses this is where meaning ends. However, for an increasing number of businesses, the leaders of these businesses are building more meaning into the work they do and in doing so, creating iconic businesses that positively serve humanity.

An iconic business is one that is in business to do more than simply make a profit. An iconic business is a place where humanity thrives because employees love working there, and society benefits more widely and appreciates what it gives back. Meaning lies at the heart of an iconic business. 'Making money' is not enough for leaders of iconic businesses. They see the world more broadly. They view the world as interconnected, with interdependencies everywhere, and for them, there is no profit in deceit. Some start off with the intention of simply making money and realise that's not enough, and others start with the question, 'How are we going to change the world for the better?' Either way it comes down to leadership and the world needs more leaders who think about the impact their company is having (or will have) on the society it serves; this is where meaning comes from, and this is the foundation on which leaders build iconic businesses of value to humanity. The purpose of a business might well be to create value and profit, the meaning of work however is to better humanity. Meaning should be core to your business. A relevant example here would be Steve Jobs, who in creating Apple, stated his mission was: 'To make a contribution to the world by making tools for the mind that advance humankind.' Or it could be part of your strategy to just do good in the world and there are a growing example of businesses doing just that:

IBM has, over recent years, placed more demand on converting its own renewable energy to the point where 37.9% of the tech company's energy use comes from renewables and they are on track to use 55% of its renewable energy by 2025.

As part of the semiconductor manufacturing process, **Intel** utilises a lot of water and recognising the need for more sustainable water usage in 2017, they have restored 80% of the water they use back into the environment, with the target being 100% by 2025.

As part of their patent strategy, **GSK** has now taken the position that it will not file drug patents in the lowest income regions across the world and they have committed to reinvesting 20% of any profits in these regions back into the training and development of health workers and medical infrastructure.

Patagonia state loudly and proudly that they are not only in the business of creating great outdoor clothing, but they also take a strong activist stance on saving the planet, to the point where they have a self-imposed Earth Tax, where the money goes to defending air, land and water around the globe.

Goldman Sachs[16] have, for over a decade, been investing capital and resources into minority-owned businesses through their '10,000 Small Businesses' program and have more recently deployed targeted capital towards communities of colour, including an additional $250 million in emergency relief to fund the Small Business Administration's Paycheck Protection Program via loans through these partners, taking their total support since the start of COVID to $1 billion. Leading from the front, David M. Solomon, Chairman and CEO and his senior team are actively redressing the balance in making sure Goldman Sachs is truly representative of humanity by creating a truly inclusive and diverse workforce.

In the social advocacy ratings, **Lego** often comes out top. Yes, the timeless maker of toy bricks from Billund in Denmark started making Lego bricks in 1932. In the World's Most Reputable Companies for Corporate Responsibility in 2019[17], Forbes ranked them number one. A business initially built purely on plastic, in 2018, it started producing pieces made from plant-based polyethylene, with an aim of making all Lego bricks sustainable by 2030.

As I write, few companies are more socially conscious than

pharmaceutical giant, **Gilead Sciences**[18]. Their total cash donation in 2015 amounted to $446.7 million (£333.2 million). Gilead's foundation is responsible for supporting many public health campaigns. Gilead is committed to widening access to healthcare and treatment, providing training programmes to health workers and working towards bridging socioeconomic healthcare barriers.

And there are many more great examples from global companies, such as Philips NV, Accenture and Nike, who not only do great and make a profit but also do good. And I also suspect if you look more closely at your local level, other smaller companies are doing their bit. One close to my heart here in the UK is **Salcombe Gin**, who use 1% profit from particular bottle sales to protect and regenerate our ocean forests – simple and yet broadens their meaning for being in business.

All of these companies place an emphasis on not only doing great but also doing good and for many of them it has been a slow transition from doing good being a small part of who they are to actually doing good becoming an integral part of who they are and how they do business.

Why are you in business?

In today's world, leaders need to be aware of the impact that both Corporate Social Responsibility (CSR) and Environmental Social Governance (ESG) are having on the way business is conducted globally. The prevailing argument that businesses should 'do good' is growing rapidly and this directly challenges Milton Friedman, who in a 1970 *New York Times* article, stated famously, or infamously (depending on your political persuasion), that the purpose of a business was to focus on and build shareholder value.

In a recent Harvard Law School post [19], institutional

investors back Friedman's claims that 'the business of business *is* business' – although in contrast, it also appears that the tide of public opinion is changing. If you were to look through the lens of financial gain when deploying a Corporate Social Responsibility (CSR) strategy, up to 87% of consumers would make a purchase based on a company's social advocacy (the act of doing good) and 78% said they would spend extra in order to do so [20]. Research also indicates a direct correlation between a company's CSR strategy and improved brand reputation, along with increased attraction and appeal of the company in the talent space, i.e., more talented people will want to join that business.

Given that there are distinct benefits to CSR, why are investors still seemingly sceptical? Having read numerous articles and research papers on this topic, there are a few reasons that stand out. First and foremost, there is the well-documented argument that few would disagree with: investors are generally interested in the short term. What is the share price today and what is it likely to be tomorrow? That metric has little bearing on whether a company adopts a CSR strategy or not.

Leaders also argue that they already 'give back' to the societies they work within, be that through the labour they provide or the time and financial funding their employees give back in their own time. It is certainly better than no activity in the CSR space, but equally, it is an argument all businesses could make in their defence. The other main reason for lack of CSR investment could also be that it is hard to measure, i.e., how can you correlate the CSR activity and an increase in revenue?

This is why Environmental Social Governance (ESG) has become more prevalent in recent years and has been more widely adopted by businesses globally.

If CSR is widely regarded as a way of making business more accountable, then ESG is more about making a business more measurable in terms of the impact the CSR strategies are having on the world. This is one of the reasons why we are beginning to see an increase in Socially Responsible Investing (SRI – also known as 'impact investing' or 'sustainable investing'). It is also widely recognised that those businesses with broader and more meaningful ESG focused attributes are more resilient to market ups and downs and are a more stable investment over a longer period of time.

Interesting origins

These are not new concepts. Socially Responsible Investing (SRI) actually dates back to John Wesley (1703-1791), one of the founders of Methodism. In one of his early sermons, he outlined the tenets of socially investing by declaring businesses should not harm their neighbours, nor take part in industries that could harm others through the chemicals they used or the products they created, like tobacco, gunpowder or alcohol. If we had fully applied his tenets to not investing back in the 1700s in such products as tobacco, gunpowder or alcohol, one wonders what the world would look like today.

The origins of ESG can be traced back to the 1970s, when a board member of General Motors, a man by the name of Reverend Leon Sullivan, created what became known as 'the Sullivan Principles'. Motivated by his abhorrence of the South African apartheid regime, these principles became the guidelines through which the US started to divest in South Africa and therefore make their views known that apartheid was a detestable practice that needed to change. Four years after Nelson Mandela was released from prison in 1994, apartheid did come to an end and social change for the good of all humanity in that beautiful country became a closer reality.

Creating meaning

The reality is leaders don't need CSR, SRI, ESG – or any other acronym for that matter – to create an iconic business. All leader's need is a wider meaning for the business they are either creating or have created. Some leaders simply create places of work that just have a much wider positive impact and I think that comes down to their point of origin.

> Some leaders ask, 'What services and products does the world need right now that I can produce and sell for a profit?'

> Other leaders ask, 'How can I make the life of humans better through the services, solutions and products I create?'

Iconic leaders focus on being of service to other humans. Their businesses become 'causes' that attract others to build something of value for humanity. They create businesses that serve humanity and, in doing so, create meaning for the humans that come to work each day for them.

> The value of work to humanity is not profit, the value of work to humanity is to make the world better than it was yesterday.

It should be the job of all leaders to create work that is meaningful beyond the numbers. We need more of these businesses in the future, more businesses that positively impact humanity, because what is good for business should also be good for humanity. We must demand a higher level of leadership thinking. No longer should we continue to accept that for some businesses, it is fine to exploit and harm humanity, otherwise we will continue to witness a never-ending battle of inequality and global instability, with businesses coming and going, with no positive impact on society other than to put a minimum wage into the 'blistered' hands of their employees and a yacht in the harbour for their executives.

Again, this is not a new idea: business serving humanity goes way back in time.

After the profound impact of the death of his brother Richard in 1899, George Cadbury (head of the Cadbury's chocolate manufacturers[21]) created the Bournville Village Trust, which consisted of 313 homes. Known as the 'Ten Shilling' or 'Sunshine Houses', these homes were set at an affordable rent to help families on low incomes. Even today, these homes, amongst many others, are still rented to people on low incomes. In fact, Bournville Village Trust manage almost 8,000 houses of mixed tenure in Bournville and other areas of Birmingham and Telford in the UK.

Andrew Carnegie, the steel tycoon, dedicated his life to philanthropy[22]. One of the many philanthropic actions he took was to build 2,509 libraries between 1883 and 1929 (1,689 were built in the United States, 660 in the United Kingdom and Ireland, 125 in Canada, and others in Australia, South Africa, New Zealand, Serbia, Belgium, France, the Caribbean, Mauritius, Malaysia, and Fiji). Carnegie built the libraries based on his belief in the power of education and subsequently, millions of people gained access to books they would never have had access to had he not invested in them. Although a plutocrat, he was also a philanthropist and by the year of his death, 1919, he had given away $350m. The UK Carnegie Trust is still improving the lives and well-being of people across the UK. Carnegie was quoted as stating: 'The man who dies rich, dies disgraced.'

Organisations that adopt a more thoughtful approach to social advocacy have undoubtedly positioned themselves to win the hearts and minds of the public. 'That is the strategic opportunity for any given business today,' Stephen Hahn-

Griffiths, leader of the Reputation Institute, says[23]. 'Explain to your community what you're doing to have a positive impact on society in a way that's unique to your organisation—that can make a huge difference.'

It's not only good for the reputational standing of the organisation. Knowing that a company you work for stands for 'doing good' will fill you and others who work for it with a sense of pride and meaning. In the future, this will become an even larger factor of attraction for potential employees. As for your need to attract 'A' players and bring in the best talent, you will need to offer a more compelling proposition than simply the work you do and the value of your share.

Giving v. Doing

Employee Supported Volunteering (ESV) programmes are on the rise. These are programmes where employees are encouraged to take a few days a year and dedicate their time not to their employer, but rather to a charity or a cause. I have been fortunate to work with companies that provide ESV time each year to all employees for them to dedicate their time to volunteering and I can attest to the fact that the level of engagement, pride and sense of achievement in these activities can be palpable. It would seem to me that more organisations should be encouraged to adopt these schemes and that local government could help set them up by providing businesses with the incentives (financial or otherwise) and support to utilise an individual's time to help ease the burden placed on the Government to 'fix' local issues. Many large and successful organisations provide meaning through philanthropy, but it is also time that is needed. Moreover, the time invested by employees breaks down societal barriers, increases awareness of others' plight and goes some way to create (through business doing good) a more diverse and inclusive world.

The power of pivoting your business

During the beginning of the COVID pandemic, we witnessed many businesses shifting their meaning for work from winning and 'profit' to 'doing good', and in doing so, created a more meaningful enterprise for their employees to belong to. Two examples that stood out for me were:

Mercedes Formula One didn't state in response to COVID that 'we just build fast racing cars'. And although the 2020 race calendar was being unpicked before their very eyes, they didn't lay off staff. The measure of their leadership was that they pivoted their business and, in collaboration with engineers from University College London, they created the UCL-Ventura breathing aid[24], a Continuous Positive Airway Pressure (CPAP) device. The device helped COVID patients with lung infections to breathe more easily, when an oxygen mask alone was insufficient. The UK Government ordered 10,000 devices and 1000 a day were produced.

Even my first beloved employer **Burberry** re-tooled their Yorkshire-based manufacturing plant and used their supply chain channels to re-purpose their workforce from making the trench coat to making surgical masks, non-surgical masks and gowns for use by medical staff and patients.

Meaning through the work you do

As a leader, if you don't have a pandemic to react to, or the means through which to create wider meaning in the social advocacy space, then, as a minimum, you still need to create meaning for your employees in the work they do.

There is still a popular view that staggers me even today and it is this 'as long as the top 50 leaders in the organisation know where the business is going, the rest will follow'. Or it is sometimes stated as 'most people don't care about what we do and why we are in business'. These statements are akin to telling a group of people who had never seen football played, or played football themselves, that when they find themselves on the pitch and ready for kick-off that all they need to do is kick the ball – how efficient and effective is that and how likely are they to succeed?

Meaning can be gained from a wider 'why' in business, external to the organisation, but it can also be associated with the way the business is led. In 1989, the Xerox Corporation were awarded the Malcolm Baldrige National Quality Award[25], which recognises US organisations in the business, healthcare, education, and non-profit sectors for performance excellence. Xerox were awarded this prestigious recognition for what was internally known as the 'Blue Book', an approach to policy deployment' (also known as Hoshin Kanri) that took the global organisational strategy and ensured that, at that time, all 80,000 employees worldwide had between 3 to 5 goals that were aligned to the global organisational strategy. This was pre-internet days, so I suspect you are thinking this was no easy task, and you would be right. But it was a strategic process which was understood in terms of the value it brought the organisation and on that basis all leaders were accountable for it. Interestingly, the Malcolm Baldrige award was not awarded because Xerox were undertaking this process; it was awarded based on how quickly the process was completed. It took 6 weeks for all 80,000 employees to agree 3 to 5 goals with their leader – 6 weeks! That's 2,666 goals every day for 6 weeks being agreed between leader and employee and at the end of it, every employee was working on something of value, something that drove business success; these were activities that created meaning. Working at Xerox in the 80s and 90s filled me with a sense of pride. We were known as a company that did things well…*really* well. Everything we did was filled with opportunities to do it even better and to this day, it influences the standards I hold of myself and others and has been a central part of the way I live my life.

Leadership in this context is about creating meaning in the work someone does, which in turn, creates alignment, engagement and a clear expectation of what is required. I mentioned that it was an agreement between the leader and employee at Xerox when the 'Blue Book' was opened, and it truly was an agreement. Xerox leaders were trained in the art of valuable conversations, where it was about building consensus to a decision. The last thing a Xerox leader would want to do is force a view (although if they had to, they would). Everything was driven by a level of consensus because the last thing we wanted in Xerox in those days were employees adopting a position of 'malicious compliance', where they would actively adopt the required action/request with the intention of proving to you that it would not work or the decision was wrong because they didn't agree. Consensus at Xerox was an outcome of everyone being heard and listened to and at the end of the discussion, an agreement was made, and even if you did not agree with it, because you had been heard and listened to and there had been debate, there was an expectation that you would support the decision. There were few egos at Xerox.

It's interesting that people refer to previous employers they have worked for as either 'they' or 'we'; however, if it's 'we', it probably indicates *even now* a deep sense of meaning and belonging created during their time with that organisation. More on belonging later.

As a Management Trainer we used to show Xerox leaders the infamous NASA video of the O-ring. On January 28, 1986, the Space Shuttle *Challenger* exploded 73 seconds after lift-off, killing seven crew members and traumatising a nation. The cause of the disaster was traced to an O-ring, a circular gasket that sealed the right rocket booster. The video re-enacts the lead up to the launch, where essentially the dynamic of 'groupthink' was created by various leaders because of the pressure within the organisational system. It is a compelling story and one NASA was keen for other global organisations to learn from. The lesson was simply this: make sure you listen to everyone so that a clear sense of meaning with everyone's full engagement is created before decisions are made.

Leadership and the creation of meaning matters. All employees should understand 'what' they're doing and 'how' it relates to the 'why' of your business. Failure to do this from a leadership perspective is a failure of leadership to ultimately engage your people. There is, of course, the other side of the argument, that is, if as a leader you cannot articulate what your people do and why, then why are they working for you?

We spelled out clearly what we required from leadership and for Xerox as a company – it was about creating meaning in the work our employees did every day. As another example, Marc Benioff's Salesforce company uses V2MOM, which stands for Vision, Values, Methods, Obstacles and Measures – few organisations do this well today and I think this has contributed to the slipping of leadership standards and an increase in short-cuts, short-termism and leadership deceit. Without everything aligned to your purpose as a leader, you face an uphill challenge in being able to deliver, so is it any wonder leaders seek alternative ways? It also contributes to a lower standard of leadership because employees cannot hold their leaders to account if they do not understand or know what is required of them and what they are ultimately striving for.

Meaning making and leadership

It's a common condition, and one that we often look on as absurd, but none-the-less, we keep doing it in business. In fact, we have been doing it for years and of late, we seem to be doing it with ever-increasing frequency. You may well be asking, 'What is this absurd act?' Well, it is the practice of appointing an employee into leadership positions because they have been a high performing employee. This is the same as promoting a person who washes dishes well to a being a Head Chef, or a good camera operator to being a newsreader. As stated earlier, leadership is not a 'position' or 'role', it is a set of specific capabilities. If people don't have these capabilities, then they should not be in a leadership position. Once you move from being an employee to a leader, you become a custodian of that business, meaning all your choices, actions and decisions should be for the benefit and value of the business. It is a set of capabilities that all too often are not made explicit when someone is recruited and appointed into a leadership role.

> The role of a leader is to create a compelling meaning for why a business exists

In the UK, the Employer skills survey (2017)[26] identified that in terms of people or personal skills found to be lacking, management and leadership skills contributed to more than half of all skills gaps (53%). Even though evidence suggests that best-practice management development (the process that leadership uses) can result in a 23% increase in organisational performance and significantly improve levels of employee engagement (source: Dept BIS), many organisations are choosing to not invest. Globally, leadership development is an industry that sees well over $350 billion invested every year, which is a significant sum, but we must be thoughtful about how and where we invest. In my experience, the higher amount of funding is spent on the more senior levels, which you can understand as there is bigger risk if the right capabilities are not evident in some of the more senior roles, however mid-level and team leadership/supervisory roles and the development of exceptional leadership in those areas has a greater impact on overall engagement, productivity and businesses performance.

Meaning creates flow

Having worked with some exceptional leaders and coaches over the years, there has been one attribute that I think sets apart the good from the great. Great leaders can make you feel that what you do counts and therefore you are valuable. I am not talking about the obligatory 'great job' or 'excellent' syndrome, where some leaders say these things almost like they have a form of Tourette's syndrome. I am talking about the way they acknowledge your work and how they make you feel when they do. They manage to create a sense that you are doing something of value and meaning and in doing so, they lift your spirit.

When work is meaningful, humans create a sense of 'flow', where time is lost. It's true, isn't it? When you are working on something meaningful and of value to you, there are three particular aspects that distinguish these activities from others:

1. Time seems to speed up, you lose a sense of time and are often left wondering, 'Where has the time gone?'
2. When you are not doing the activity, you miss it and long to be doing it again.
3. No matter how much time you spend on it, you never tire of it.

This third point is interesting in the context of work. How many of us go home tired and fatigued from the work we do? How many of us go on holiday for a rest because we are tired of work, thinking that a 'rest will do us good', only to go back to work and within two weeks feel like we need another break?

The antidote to exhaustion, fatigue and sheer lack of resilience is not 'rest', despite what we would like to think, it is not to stay 'under the duvet'. The antidote is to wholeheartedly live a life with meaning. In my experience,

I become more resilient when I care about what I do and who I am doing it with and for. For all of us, life can seem like an endless stream of (how Churchill defined 'history') 'one bloody problem after the other' but our ability to rise and overcome is where resilience resides and meaning exists. We all have it within us, because the chances are you are not reading this under your duvet.

> Resilience: (Noun) the capacity to recover quickly from difficulties, toughness

Resilience is a word that has crept into organisational life and yet, I must be honest, my initial reaction to it was one of rejection. My rejection of the word 'resilience' as a way of defining a critical new attribute came from this: why would we as leaders create a workplace where people had to be resilient to do their best work? Surely a business, at least a well-oiled one, would be a slick and efficient operation, where the only challenge is to keep up with the pace and speed at which it operates? Let's face it, who among us would apply for a role that started in the job ad, 'Come join us - we'll *really* grow your resilience'? It is not an attribute most of us would go out of our way to deliberately develop.

My thinking recently, certainly since COVID has graced our lives, has changed. I still think 'resilience' jars with what it really means to operate a business effectively, but you and I are members of humanity, and let's be honest, things are a little tough right now! For me, being resilient is simple; it means 'no matter what, you get out of bed every day and do what is necessary', but you and I know that can be tough at times. The longer you live, the chances are there will be times when staying under the warm duvet is going to be a far more attractive proposition. No one is exempt from these days and if they say they are, they are lying.

I do not have the answer for what sense of meaning taps into your resilience. You do. I hope it is your work and if it's not, you find it somewhere else and soon. All I know is that your ability to 'get up' is your 'first base', so notice the days when the duvet is lighter; what interests you and excites you and what do you care about? What nourishes and sustains you? Find ways of bringing more of those days into your weekly schedule as these will provide the fuel and fire for the days when the duvet is heavy. And finally, be kind to yourself and others, we all have 'off' days, so be there for those who fall so you can help them get up, it might be the very reason you will feel the need to get up tomorrow.

A better day

While working as a performance coach for a trading floor of a global Fortune 100 energy company, I coached the Chief Legal Officer (CLO). She had an impressive office overlooking St Paul's in the heart of the City of London. Her office was as impressive as she was. A glittering career, high intellect coupled with high emotional intelligence, formed a potent mix. We established a strong relationship over the first few sessions, where we discussed various tactical matters that were bothering her at the time, but as I got to know her, the more I felt something wasn't quite right.

I still vividly remember the day when we were again talking tactics and she stopped and looked at me, and with tears clearly forming in her eyes, she told me, 'I am not happy here'. I remember processing the statement and thinking that the word 'here' was worthy of further exploration. 'Where would you be happy?' I asked.

Cutting a long story short, her story is not unusual. You may know the story yourself, or you may know of a friend or colleague who is the central character in this common 'play'. The script goes something like this: growing up, this person loved art and music, in fact they were pretty good at it and enjoyed these activities very much, but their parents had other ideas. Wanting to please and not let the parents down, the person forgot about what they enjoyed doing and went to university, then law school and became a lawyer. The parents were very proud, and this person loved making them proud. The career blossomed and this person became an exceptional corporate lawyer and initially enjoyed the recognition, pay, perks and the lifestyle that came with it. Eventually, they became a Chief Legal Officer for a Fortune 100. Midlife quickly arrived and one morning, this person finds themselves tired and worn out on the London tube with fellow commuters and suddenly wonders, 'Why am I doing this?' It doesn't take this person long to recognise that the answer to the question is 'my parents', and this makes them sad; sad that they did not choose their own career, sad they have lost time, sad they are not doing work that is meaningful to them.

Meaning and Reverse Engineering

I remember once meeting Andy, a management consultant who I did some associate work for, and as a younger aspiring freelance management consultant, he seemed to be living a 'good life'. We hit it off immediately and he became my mentor in the early days of my first dive into freelance work. He loved to sail and owned a racing yacht that we used for team building events and he also loved to paint; he was quite an artist. He never worked more than 3 days a week because, as he put it, 'I have too many other things I love to do'.

His life and the way he had created it was a mystery to me and the more I spent time with him, the more curious I became. One day, after dropping off a team we had been working with that day in the English Channel, we were taking the boat back up the Hamble Estuary to Hythe. As the sun was setting on what was another great day exploring team dynamics on a racing yacht, I remember sitting with him at the stern and asking him how he got to where he was now. His answer was compelling, and I'll never forget it. He went on to say that he was invited by his parents at the age of 16 to describe (through his art) what a 'perfect day' would be when he was 40. He drew boats, houses on the water, family, cars, friends, barbecues on the beach, pictures in a gallery (he sold his paintings as another form of income), all of which he said represented his life now. It turned out the reason for his life now representing the paintings he had drawn as a 16-year-old was that, after an enthusiastic few days of painting, his mother and father reviewed his work and then asked him this question, 'What are you going to do for a living that will give you those things in your life?'

> The quality of the questions you ask helps to build the quality of your life.

His parents (probably unknowingly) had helped him 'reverse engineer' his life. Not only did he create a great company that worked in leadership and organisational development, but he also created a life he wanted to live; a life that gave him meaning. Andy was someone who inspired others to do good. We once raised over £3000 for my village hall's refurbishment simply by donating his yacht, *Esprit de Corps*, for a team-building event in the English Channel.

What do these stories have to do with organisations and meaning? I think organisations ruthlessly squander human capability by not exploring how a person could be of more use to the enterprise. It is the leader's job to find out what their people enjoy and like doing and in so doing bring more meaning to the work they do. Key questions to ask could include:

a) What have you enjoyed over the past week or month?
b) What would you like to do more of in the future?

c) How can I help as your leader?

These three questions are powerful ways in which leaders can bring meaning back into one's work. Plus, if people like doing something, they are more likely to be good at it. It is also worth noting that you, as a leader, need to be able to answer these questions too and so bring more meaning into *your* life, so that you too are fuelled for the days ahead.

The Black Swan

Businesses, by nature, serves. The opportunity facing humanity now is to widen the spectrum of the service business provides and in doing so, increase humanity's meaning and value derived from work. Businesses typically serve their customers and shareholders, then perhaps their employees, and if they have anything left to give, society, and normally in that order of priority (sometimes it is the shareholder first). This order is attached to the outdated mantra of business being for the purposes of profit, i.e., serve your customers and that in turn serves the business because it brings in revenue. In a world of growing inequality, that's simply no longer enough.

The 'Black Swan'[27] of this pandemic may not be the pandemic itself but the impact it is going to have on our society from this day forward. There will be a more prominent role for businesses to support the societies they serve. Governments would be well advised to explore how they could support businesses in becoming socially conscious and therefore, doing more in the communities and societies they serve. Business schools could start to look at how they bring this level of leadership into the school curriculum. Think about how powerful it would be if governments had more multinationals to support the societies they serve, and in doing so, increased the meaning of work for their employees. Business leaders could be doing this through increased time for volunteering, short-term hire policies[28] (e.g., hiring Armed Forces personnel), stronger links with local educational authorities and NGOs, and incentives to invest and build labour for required sectors and economies such as the green economy, and all the while creating greater meaning for the existence of their business.

Social change is already being influenced by the way big businesses operate and soon this level of expectation and scrutiny will be spread across the business spectrum, regardless of the size of the business or the sector the business is in. Leaders not only need to understand this as a requirement, but they also need to be educated in how this could provide opportunity for greater levels of business success.

As previously mentioned, the degree of transparency that is increasing daily, via websites such as Glassdoor and Comparably et al. (these are websites where current, or past employees, can write reviews about what it was like to work in the companies they have worked for), means that potential employees can be more aware about their choices of employment. Previous to Glassdoor and Comparably and the like, substantial reputational damage for business misdemeanours would mainly be through the press and there was no significant accountability for organisations to change – but now there is. Since the advent of the likes of Glassdoor and Comparably, there is also a lower tolerance in society for organisations that openly exploit the 'system'. It is not right that in the 21st century there are still organisations out there that act unscrupulously, whether it be from the way they organise their business to avoid paying tax, or the fact they are still exploiting human labour or working conditions. To address this, we must raise society's awareness and expectation of leadership and sites like Glassdoor and Comparably are doing exactly that.

Meaning is the starting point for any iconic business. It is the centre of gravity through which all the other aspects of building an exceptional business become reality. We (i.e. leadership development practitioners, consultants, business schools, local governments) must do more to help leaders of businesses think more broadly about creating meaning because this is how we create more economic and societal value from work.

Meaning is the fuel that humanity needs to prosper. Helping people to do something of intrinsic value and meaning to them has been proven to increase an individual's self-esteem and mental health. Work should be one such activity.

In summary: questions, provocations and actions to increase meaning:

- What does your business stand for?
- What does an iconic business mean to you and how will it be expressed in the leadership you bring to the world and the legacy you leave?
- What is the extent of your leadership ambition?
- What will be your leadership legacy?
- What could you give back to the communities and countries you serve?
- To what degree do you focus on creating a business that is truly meaningful?
- Strategy and an employee's understanding of it should be explained in the time it takes to view a TikTok – how easily is your strategy understood within your organisation?
- Are you solving or creating problems for humanity?
- How motivational is your business to work for?

Actions

- Survey your employees to understand how meaningful work is for them and explore how you could make it more fulfilling.

- Choose a global or local charity you will actively support as a business and set a target on how much funding you will raise or hours you will provide in support of the charity each year.
- There is only one 'priority' — when you have '*priorities* – plural' you simply have a list of things to do. And nobody likes a list of things to do! Have one priority (one reason to exist) that creates meaning, focus and commitment in your organisation. Don't print it on a small card, simply encourage your people to tell everyone about it.
- Set up an Employee Supported Volunteering (ESV) programme that provides time for your employees to dedicate their support to a charity or NGO close to their heart.
- Support your employees with mentoring and coaching so they can explore how to create greater meaning in the work they do in their life, either with you, or with another employer or a self-employed career.
- Ask your employees what they enjoy about their work and what would they like to do more of. This may open up areas of their work that you can amplify in making them of even more value to the overall team or organisational success.
- Search for opportunities to link your business with your local communities, or to a cause greater than your own, and search for ways in which you can support it, either through offering your employees' time, expertise or through funding.

Chapter Four: Growth instead of decay

I am sure I am not the only one who, every time I go to an inspiringly good theatre show, where I have been wooed and wowed by the characters in the show, I come out and have a level of envy for the actors in the play, who for two plus hours have made us laugh, cry and applaud and ultimately left feeling better as a human. You probably remember that feeling of being inspired and uplifted that leaves you with a sense of curiosity and hope for the future. 'Oh, how I would love to do that job' – to have the impact that makes *that many people* feel optimistic, heartened and good, *every day*! As I stand and applaud, I find myself thinking, 'What a job…'

Well, that is our job as a leader.

As leaders, I also know that is not our day-to-day reality and yet, we should not stop striving to achieve more of those days when the people who work with us go home to their families, satisfied and fulfilled, in knowing that they did good work that day. As leaders, we are ultimately in the human growth game. If the people who work for us grow, so does our business.

The truth here is that people *choose* to work for you. It is also true that organisations are messy and getting things done can be difficult, but the role of the leader is to make it as easy as possible for humans to bring and do their best, as well as grow – every day. All too often, reading the manual to a space rocket would be easier than understanding any business operating model. Reporting lines, matrices, systems, processes, centralised v. de-centralised operating models, restrained or unclear budgets, internal v. external, agile v. stable, policies, delegation of authority, regulations, audits – the list can be never-ending and it would seem that the job of leadership in an organisation is to either fix, delete, install or simplify these hurdles so individuals can, at a minimum, feel they have some chance of doing what is necessary.

Going into the future, I fully suspect work will still have all the trappings of the bygone age of business: i.e., processes, policies, delegation of authority,etc, but what will become vital is how they work effectively together to enhance organisational performance. How do they enable the human element of the organisation to come together, to collaborate, to innovate and problem-solve? Speed will be the differentiator in business growth and success and the systems that were used 20 years ago can now be more easily integrated due to Application Programming Interfaces (API) and this trend is set to continue giving businesses stronger I.T. system platforms through which to provide a more bespoke and user-centric experience and so provide rich data and insights, leading to more efficient ways of working at pace.

In the past, businesses purchased systems to automate most processes and going forward, these needs will still be the same, but the emphasis will also be on creating an ecosystem of I.T. platforms that intelligently provide easy access to valuable and powerful data, which can be used to enhance business performance.

The Human v. The Organisation

There seems to be two sides to performance. On the one side, you have the organisation itself and on the other, the human. It is widely recognised and understood that 70% of an individual's performance is based on the environment leaders place them in, i.e., is it easy to do their work and are they well-led?

Look for deviants

When leading people, the first question to ask as a leader is, 'do people have the resources they need to do what is expected in the role?' The second question is, 'how easy is it for an individual to get things done around here?' If it is difficult, then your job as their leader is to make it easier, but this is not always easy, so as a leader, how do you do this? At times, it is difficult to see the wood for the trees in an organisation. Whenever I coach leaders on this subject, I often ask, 'are all your people underperforming?' and the answer that comes back is, 'Well, of course *not all* are underperforming'. That means there are 'positive deviants' in your midst and this is fertile ground and here is why.

The term 'positive deviance' was coined by Jerry and Monique Sternin, who worked with Save the Children in Vietnam in the 1990s, a country at that time still ravished by high levels of infant death, disease, and malnourishment. Jerry and Monique were sent by Save the Children to fix the problem. The story goes that when they stepped off the plane, the local Save the Children Ambassador was there to meet them and told them that they immediately had many villages to visit and that they were in desperate need of their help, to which Jerry replied, 'Don't take me there, take me to see the villages where there is no infant death, disease or malnourishment'. What Jerry was looking for were those exceptions to the rule. Those exceptions where, despite all the challenges and hurdles, individuals and communities who were not only coping *but thriving*. In Jerry and Monique's case, after observing these villages, they witnessed that the children were fed what many would deem unsuitable food and yet it was highly nutritious (crab, shrimp and sweet potato), they washed their hands and their children's hands before mealtimes and fed them three meals a day. Small things that made a big difference to child nutrition, health and well-being. Observing these habits, Jerry and Monique were then able to go to the other villages with sadly greater amounts of disease and malnourishment and resourcefully help them overcome their challenges.

When building growth in organisations, a useful question to ask is, 'when or where is it *not* a problem?' Assuming there will be different degrees to a problem, go to where it is less of a problem and study and observe what makes it so. You'll then be better able to resolve the organisational problem more resourcefully and increase performance and thus provide a sense of achievement and growth for your employees.

The Road to Hell

I remember reading about the 'M25'. The M25 is the motorway that encircles London. London is roughly 45 miles wide, so it was rightly named the world's biggest roundabout. In its early days, it was a horrid road to be on; always blocked and jammed. It was so bad it even inspired Chris Rea to write a song about it – *The Road to Hell*. A great song about a horrible road.

Why am I telling you this? You may rightfully be asking. Well, there is a particular stretch that links two motorways, the M4 to the M3, two of the main artery roads into and out of London. It goes past London Heathrow's access to Terminal 5 (the home of British Airways) and for many years, in the 90s and 2000s, it was constantly being worked on and extended, i.e., 3 lanes to 4, 4 lanes to 5, etc. Numerous lanes were added until they ran out of room to put any more in and yet the problem of traffic jams did not abate. Until one day, when someone asked a different question, 'When are traffic jams less of a problem?' An interesting question to explore. It turns out that counter to intuition, more traffic flowed on the M25 between the M4 and M3 when the roadworks *were in place*. It turned out that dictating slower speeds kept a consistent flow of traffic running without jamming up the roads. Today the M25 has speed-related signs that are enforced to keep everyone to a certain speed and subsequently fewer traffic jams occur – a problem solved by simply asking a different question – when is it less of a problem?

Small things matter

As with most things in life, it is the small things that matter. Back in 2002, when Sir David Brailsford took over British Cycling, they had won only one gold medal in a 76-year history. Roll forward to the 2008 Beijing Olympics and Britain won 7 out of a possible 10 gold medals. By anyone's standards, that's pretty impressive, so what happened? Sir David focused on what he termed 'marginal gains'. As an MBA student, he had become obsessed with the theory of Kaizen. Kaizen, interestingly, was at the heart of the Xerox culture in the 80s and 90s: a ruthless pursuit of 'progression rather than perfection', with the focus on the 1%: i.e., if you broke down riding a bike at speed into a 100 x 1%'s and then looked to improve each 1%, you would radically shift the level of performance. To give you a few examples of the level of detail Sir David would go to, he and his team identified improvements in the following:

- Massage gel that was used for muscle recovery was analysed for its effectiveness and new gels were used and adopted that had a better impact on recovery time.
- Dust hindered bike performance so the truck labs that followed the bikes around and where the bikes were fixed were painted white to highlight any dust and help keep the place clean.
- Riders had their sleep mattresses and pillows they used at home replicated on tour so they had the same level of sleep quality when they were in competition.

Another good example of an athlete who applied a marginal gains approach to growth was Michael Johnson. Once asked whether he could run faster after breaking the 400m world record he emphatically stated: 'Yes.' When asked how he knew this by some bemused members of the press, he responded by stating he had freeze-framed every running step during the successful record attempt and said that his '63rd step had landed weak', and that's why he knew he could run faster. He had created a habit of videoing and freeze-framing the impact of each running step during the race to see how he could improve. His perfect race was built on many aspects, one of them being the correct impact of his feet on the track when at speed.

Small things matter and iconic businesses build routines and practices that, on the face of it, seem meaningless to the outsider but internally, they define the company culture and are there to bring out the best in their people every day. At Xerox, we used Kaizen reviews for the last 5 minutes of *every* meeting. 'What went well?' and 'How can we improve?' were the two central questions we focused on. What does your business do as a routine that sets you up for growth and further success?

> What are your growth routines?
>
> What are you doing today that ensure you and the people you lead are better tomorrow?

I believe in you

At its core, growth is based on trust. We call it something fancier nowadays: 'psychological safety' but it means the same thing. It refers to that feeling you have that bad things will not happen if I fail or say something contentious or stupid in a certain environment. As humans, we are all a 'work in progress' so it's part of our nature that we fail – that's how we grow. It is also true that we sometimes need people around us to believe in us; to say 'you can do this'. As a leader, we need to have trust that people will do their best and when it doesn't quite work out, help them find even betters ways for next time.

As a leader never underestimate the impact you have on another's performance. I can still vividly remember *being trusted* and the way it made me feel and what it did to my confidence, development and ultimately, my career. At Xerox I was on what was called 'management track', which was a process of leadership development followed by committee reviews to ensure you were ready for your first management position. As a young man, I was filled with insecurities (I still am) about whether I could be a good leader and my mentor was a guy by the name of Lee Adams. Lee was a cockney who was full of confidence and what he lacked in university education, he made up with sheer wit, cunning and intelligence. He was a big man with a big heart, and he wasn't afraid to show it. As my mentor, he was challenging and supportive in equal measure, which, as we will cover later in the book, are the two main cornerstones to human growth.

I remember a week where I was shadowing Lee prior to him going off on holiday and as part of my development, I would stand in for him while he was off. He had a big role; thousands of customers, a multi-million (£) P&L and a huge budget to manage, so you can imagine as a young aspiring leader, this was all quite daunting. While shadowing Lee one day, we had a customer review meeting scheduled with a key client in Bristol, England. I had heard through 'word of mouth' that this customer was not one of the easiest clients to deal with and when the client showed up with an entourage of legal representatives and account leaders and started to tell Lee in no uncertain terms how unhappy he was with the levels of service, the prediction of not being easy to deal with became reality. I watched as Lee took in all he was ranting about while taking notes and asking questions for clarity at points that did not interrupt the client's flow. Over time, the client's anger and frustration lessened. At around the 30-minute mark, the client laughed at Lee's wit, at 45 minutes they had agreed a way forward, and at 55 minutes, they were talking about holidays and rounds of golf, and on the hour, they left the building, with smiles all round. I was in awe! I was also filled with a huge sense of dread. What would I have done had I been in Lee's chair, and *I would be in his chair* the following week while he was on holiday.

Filled with awe, self-doubt and bewilderment as to how Lee had handled the meeting, I asked him, 'How did you do that?' 'Do what?' Lee responded. 'How did you manage to bring that customer round?' I asked again, seeking further clarity on what 'training course' he went on or 'book' he had read so I could cram them into my development, so I would be ready for the following week. Now to this day, I am not sure whether what he eventually said to me was calculated or just a throwaway response. I'd like to think he knew the impact he was going to have on me, because what he eventually replied with was an eight-word sentence. A sentence that I can honestly say has significantly influenced and shaped my professional life and continues to do so today. Lee replied, 'If I can do it, so can you'. Here was a man I respected and admired saying that I could do what he did. That's trust. I didn't need to be provided with another course or book title, I needed someone to show confidence and belief in me, and in that short sentence. he gave it to me. 'If I can do it, so can you' – not every leader who says that to a person who works with them will have the same impact, only those who are trustworthy.

As a slight aside, I remember being in a taxi in Louisville, Kentucky and I was talking to Jack, my taxi driver about the greatest fighter of all time – Muhammed Ali. Jack told me that when he was young, Ali used to frequently burst into his Louisville primary schools, strategically timed, when all the kids were in assembly and you would hear him at the top of his voice chanting, 'I AM THE GREATEST,' over and over as he walked down the corridor, getting louder and louder as he approached the assembly hall. The kids would be shaking with excitement and anticipation of seeing their hero. Then (still ranting), he would enter the assembly hall and walk up to the podium and shout the loudest, 'I AM THE GREATEST.' Then when everyone was listening, in a quieter tone, looking the kids in the eyes, he would point to them and say: 'And you could be too'.

> If you want people to grow, your belief in them is the most precious of gifts.

Business is conducted via relationships and it is the strength of these relationships that determines the quality of the work and the value of the output. If we trust others, they will bring more of themselves to work, express their views and challenge others more because they know they all have each other's backs. It should not be any surprise that the world's greatest teams, be those in the boardroom, sports fields, schools, colleges, universities or the military, have high levels of trust between its team members.

If leaders are trusted, their people will walk through walls for them, and they will do it willingly because they know that the leader has respect, care and good intentions towards them and will ultimately fight their corner if, and when, it is needed. As we go through this book, you should start to form your own view of what leadership is because to create an iconic business or team, you need great leadership. *You* need to be a better leader tomorrow than you are today. You are either growing as a leader or not and if not, the impact on your business will be decay. Over the years, I have come to realise that leadership can be 'felt'. When you are around 'it', you feel inspired. When you look back and reflect on your life, these leaders are remembered. You recall their names because deep in the recesses of your memory, they made you feel valued and cared for, you learnt from them and you held respect for them. We search for these people and remember their names because subconsciously we never know when we may need them.

> Do you remember working for, or being in the presence of someone who inspired you?
>
> Who were they and what made them stand out from others?
>
> What routines or attributes do you need to adopt to create higher levels of trust with the people you lead?

Building growth through clear communication

As leaders, we are all too often not clear in our communication. We try to use metaphor or narrative to be clever in the way we engage with others, only to switch off and or confuse the people we lead. We use terms like 'freedom within a framework', which is paradoxical and yet this is the space in which leaders operate. We want people to feel free to do what is necessary, but employees will need to know what 'free' is and where the 'constraints' are, so give examples of where there are defined limits and boundaries. Encourage them to find the constraints, to test the boundaries and in doing so, define them so they become even more suitable to how you need to work. Your employees will only do this if they firstly feel encouraged to do so and secondly, have the skills to be able to navigate these grey areas. Competing goals and conflicting reward schemes often stop leaders from collaborating to overcome a particular problem within the framework. Great leadership that builds trust is about setting the goal and the parameters and then getting out of the way so that your people can do what is necessary to succeed and bring about the right performance outcome.

A good example of a leader who set the parameters and then

removed themselves from the situation happened on the morning of the 30 April 1980, when a group of six armed men stormed the Iranian embassy in Prince's Gate in South Kensington, London. The terrorists were members of the Arab KSA group and were demanding sovereignty of a southern Iranian region. They took 26 people hostage and demanded the release of prisoners from prisons in Khuzestan, as well as their own safe passage out of the UK. If their demands were not met, then they would start to kill hostages. Margaret Thatcher, the then UK Prime Minister, held daily Cabinet Office Briefing Room (COBR) meetings to be kept abreast of the situation. The story goes that Margaret Thatcher (recognising she quite rightly did not have the skills to negotiate or deal with a terrorist hostage situation) brought the head of the Metropolitan Police Force (London Police) and the Head of the UK Armed Forces together and set out the following three parameters:

a. We must do all we can to bring about a peaceful end to this situation.
b. These terrorists must *not* leave the country and must be held to account for their crimes on UK soil.
c. And finally, if we lose the life of one hostage, we must use all the available force necessary to bring the situation to an immediate close.

On day five of the siege, at 13:45 GMT, Abbas Lavasani, the embassy's chief press officer was taken downstairs and executed. At 19:23, two SAS teams stormed the Embassy, freeing the hostages and killing all but one terrorist and bringing an end to the siege.

Never mix capability with performance

There is a myth in business that when you are measuring a person's performance, you are measuring their capability – this is not true. Performance and capability are not the same thing. 'Capability' is dependent on not only that person's knowledge, skill and understanding, but also on the processes, systems, resources and culture around the person that supports their ability to perform.

Think about it this way. Setting a goal for someone who is very capable, and the goal is clearly unachievable is a sure-fire way of either switching them off, or burning them out. The other aspect that many organisations don't seem to understand is that you can have exceptional human performance and yet still not meet the target, succeed and win. This is true in sports, and it is true in business. Reasons for this can be complex but the two main reasons are either the target is set is too high, or the wrong target has been set.

> As a leader do you accept the targets were too high and too demanding, or do you castigate the individual for not achieving them?

Most leaders would not accept that the target was too high. Some may even leave it there, hoping 'if they try hard enough, it may still be a good level of achievement', with no thought as to whether it will burn the individual out. There may also be exceptions, i.e., a 'positive deviant' who hit the target and *didn't* burn him or herself out in the pursuit of achieving it.

> Don't manage performance, manage the growth of the human and remember you don't buy talent, you buy history

One common myth is that 'we can hire those people in' but this can be a dangerous and a highly costly exercise that can often backfire. How many times have you seen, on the face of it, very talented people with proven track records in winning, being brought into an organisation, only to see them fail? You see it in sports, as well as organisations. Why is this? I think the culture (which goes back to the environment) has a lot to do with whether this new employee will perform or not. Analyse the individual you are looking to hire, not so much through their experience but through the lens of how they would fit in your current culture. If they come from a workplace that did things differently, and your culture and ways of working are quite the opposite, how realistic is it that they will perform? They may have the capabilities to do the job *but not* the capabilities in the context of your culture. Very quickly these talented employees fall back on the excuse, 'we didn't do it this way'. To grow and succeed your hiring strategy, coupled with your brand identity and reputation, will to a large extent, ensure you bring in the right people who will be driven to achieve.

> Experience does not determine competence.

There is another common myth: experience equals competence. I am afraid this is not true either. If it were, those that have been driving 20 years would be better drivers than those that had been driving 3 years. It is not the years of experience that determines a level of achievement, it is the experience within those years! How much has that person pursued new experiences, failed and challenged their own knowledge, been curious to study beyond their given field of so-called expertise and how much have they practiced and researched their field of study? All these aspects go towards determining whether they will grow and achieve in a role and if so, to what degree.

If you want to win, you must have the 'right players on the field' and in my experience, leaders can sometimes be so keen to hire the person, it feels like the only legitimate requirement for that hire is that they can 'fog a mirror'. *Never* compromise, it is better to wait to get the right hire, than to potentially hire the wrong person.

'Are you looking for talent that will hit targets others have yet to hit, or genius that hits targets others are yet to see?'

Schopenhauer

For senior appointments in organisations, are you looking for someone with confidence to do a great job, or are you looking for a maverick who will view the situation with new eyes and potentially create something very different? If you want to become an iconic business that outperforms your competitors, you need to create a brand identity that attracts the right people who want to come and work for you and a hiring strategy that forensically sorts the wheat from the chaff. And finally, remember that poor hiring decisions damage the reputation, morale, achievement, and performance of your organisation – so it is vital you do it right.

Once you have the right hires, how do you keep them motivated to commit and grow in your organisation? Although a healthy turnover is 10% of your workforce each year, challenges in retention and attrition are problems many organisations face. How do we keep and grow the employees we need each year and slow down extremes in employee churn?

Recognise results – Appreciate effort

One of the distinctions of an iconic business is they reward their people, but they do it in a way that creates continued motivation to do what they have been rewarded for. It seems odd, doesn't it, that you would be less motivated to do something based on being rewarded for doing it? But it can, and often happens, and here is why.

Great leaders realise that the 'golden rule' does not apply when leading others. The 'golden rule' simply states that 'you should treat people the way you would like to be treated'. Now, as a starting point, this is fine, because we are all rational, kind and compassionate people (well most of us). And if we act that way to others, it generally works out fine. That said, if we apply the same way *we* would like to be recognised to all we meet, then we will come up short as their leader. I am sure you have come across some people who when you have given them positive recognition for a job well done, they simply say, 'Well, that's what you pay me for.' That may, in fact, be you. They seem to brush it off, almost embarrassed that they have been recognised in the first place. Equally, I am sure you have also come across some people who go out of their way to request feedback on a piece of work and get frustrated when all you say is 'thanks for your contribution' or 'great effort'.

> Great leaders are curious and consistently pursue ways in which to find out what motivates their inner value system and that of those around them.

There are some people who place an emphasis on what they have done. The result, achievement, or output; an innovative idea, or creation, the solving of a challenge. For these people, it is not about 'how' they have achieved something, but the fact that they did. Recognising the output, the result, the achievement meets their inner value system for being 'recognised' in terms of what they have done in work or in life. The differences are in some ways subtle and yet in other ways, very pronounced.

Recognition: focuses on the achievement, the outcome and the result

Appreciation: focuses on the personal attributes e.g. dedication, care, commitment etc

I have two beautiful daughters (now young women), Aleena and Darcey, and when they were growing up, I'd come home from work and have that wonderful welcome in the summer holidays of all their artwork being presented to you to be judged accordingly. We would sit down and Darcey would almost throw her pictures at me pointing at them, and saying, 'Look at this, Daddy,' and I'd say (before I knew about this), 'You are so clever.' And she'd say, pointing at the picture, 'What about this?' and 'Look have you seen that?' She was guiding me to what she wanted to hear me say: 'What a great picture'. It wasn't about how clever she was, it was all about the output for Darcey. Aleena, on the other hand, would hold the picture close to her and say to me, 'What do you think of this?' (really, what she was asking was 'What do you think of me?'), and I'd say (sadly again before I knew about this), 'What a great picture.' And she'd respond, 'But what about this and this and this?' It wasn't until I pointed out how clever she was or what a creative artist she was that the request for feedback would subside and her little back would stiffen and with a sense of pride, she would walk off saying to herself, 'Yes I am clever and a great artist.' The interesting conclusion to this little foray into my inadequate fathering techniques is that Aleena went to Gloucester University to study Editorial & Advertising and in her first year, she was finding things quite difficult. The reason was that all the lecturers were critiquing her work and things did not change until we had a conversation around 'you're *good* enough, otherwise you wouldn't have been accepted on to the programme and the lecturers are not there to make you feel good about yourself, they are there to make you a *great* editorial photographer and in doing so, ensure you pass the degree and find gainful employment'. The lecturers focused on the result, not on the personal characteristics that created the work, i.e., effort, dedication, commitment etc., and the lack of attribute-led feedback (e.g., you are really strong in this area, you have a great eye for creativity etc) was starting to erode Aleena's self-confidence and belief.

Over a period of a good few years, I worked with Andy Vass, a well-respected and prominent Leadership Coach and Behavioural Management specialist in the education sector. Andy and I had worked across many of the Scottish Education Executive's authorities, working with heads and principal teachers and the idea behind the work was simply this: if teachers learnt and coached each other in the staffroom, then the level of learning in the classroom would increase. A simple and yet compelling hypothesis, which we both had the opportunity to test out. There were many memorable moments during the years Andy and I worked together, but one in particular stands out for me, and it was based around the idea that we should recognise results and appreciate effort.

Andy and I ran the session in Edinburgh with around 50 headteachers and principals and over a period of an hour, had them starting to recognise the differences between recognising results and appreciating effort. When we looked at the group, at least 70% had a need for being appreciated for their personal attributes, and the discussion became quite heated and animated when they started to talk about Her Majesty's Inspectorate of Education (HMIe), an executive agency of the Scottish Government, responsible for the inspection of public and independent, primary and secondary schools. Now HMIe had been criticised over the years for being heavily biased towards the numbers element in terms of measuring educational performance, even though the intent is a positive one to ensure high standards of education; so why is it that a teacher's view of an HMIe review was often a negative one? It became apparent that many teachers go into the teaching profession to help children and so have a positive impact on their life, and yet their schools are assessed and recognised for the standards of education in terms of how many A's they have as a percentage of the pupil population. There is a disconnect between what HMIe values and what teachers view as being 'valuable'. For teachers, it's about how much they improve the learning of those that are below standards by caring for their education, taking time with them and listening, questioning and challenging them to do more than what they think they are capable of achieving. For HMIe, it was the percentage of grades that were attained. The footnote to this example is that over recent years, HMIe have certainly started to balance how they view and determine educational excellence so that it captures the inputs and outputs of a school's performance more accurately.

Another example would be healthcare workers, who face a similar dilemma. They go into the profession to care for and help other humans recover from illness. The measures they are judged on in the UK by the Care Quality Commission (CQC) are: levels of safety, effectiveness, care, responsiveness and leadership. At the time of writing, there are over 1227 independent hospital care premises at over 2767 locations, of which only 7% have achieved 'outstanding'. 95% of all Primary Medical Services did not achieve 'outstanding'. Low levels of staffing, lack of resources and in some public cases, poor leadership, are often cited as the reason for this level of performance. We have set the National Health Service up to fail and yet the sheer fact it doesn't is because of the hard work, dedication, commitment and loyalty of its exceptional staff who care.

The point here is that the measure on which you review performance should *recognise* not only the level of achievement (e.g., bed availability, number of A's, revenue, profit, EBITDA, levels of service etc.), it should also *appreciate* the human attributes so often ignored and yet required to deliver results (e.g., time with patients, smiles and levels of positivity, care, learning, commitment, time with students, listening, challenging, supporting, coaching, mentoring others etc.). This would mean a more humanistic view of performance that would ensure that those in certain professions were valued for their contribution to the organisations and societies they serve, as well as the results they achieve.

An interesting result of the visible appreciation shown to the healthcare workers at the beginning of the pandemic (in the UK and many European countries, every Thursday at 20:00, the public showed their appreciation by standing on their porch and clapping) was that the number of applications from people wanting to work in the NHS increased. In March 2020, there were 407,000 applications for 27,700 jobs that were advertised in that month[29]. Similar trends were seen in the US, where, as well as healthcare workers, there was also a focus on e-commerce roles, ranging from warehouse to delivery drivers. Of course, partly this is driven by need, but could it also be because these roles were in demand and were being appreciated by those millions of us who had to stay in lockdown and rely on care.

> Culture is core to human growth and achievement and, in case you did not know, as a leader, you set the culture through the tone of your leadership.

We stated earlier that the environment contributes to about 80% of a person's performance, so culture matters. Culture is your differentiator, i.e., how it feels to work with you, do work with you and be served by your services and products will determine how people perform and that is obviously linked to whether your customers will return and remain loyal to you. At GlaxoWellcome, we worked closely with Boston Consulting Group back in the late 90s, on the merger of two of the world's biggest pharmaceutical companies (GlaxoWellcome and SmithKline Beecham) to form GSK, and we took culture seriously. Our mantra was that we brought together 'the best of both' cultures to create an exceptional pharmaceutical company. We employed the help of the then Strathclyde University professor, Gerry Johnson and the Cultural Web[30] that both Gerry and Kevan Scholes created in 1992. The Cultural Web identifies six interrelated elements that help to make up what Johnson and Scholes call the 'paradigm' – the pattern or model – of the work environment. By analysing the factors in each, you can begin to see what makes up the landscape of your culture: what is working, what is not, and what needs to be changed.

The six elements are:

- **Stories** – The past events and the people who are talked about inside and outside the company. Who and what the company chooses to immortalise says a great deal about what it values and perceives as great behaviour.
- **Rituals and Routines** – The daily behaviour and actions of people that signal acceptable behaviour. This determines what is expected to happen in given situations, and what is valued by management.
- **Symbols** – The visual representations of the company, such as logos, how plush the offices are, and the formal or informal dress codes.
- **Organisational Structure** – This includes both the structure defined by the organisation chart, and the unwritten lines of power and influence that indicate whose contributions are most valued.
- **Control Systems** – The ways that the organisation is controlled. These include financial systems, quality systems, processes and policies and rewards (including the way they are measured and distributed within the organisation).
- **Power Structures** – The pockets of *real* power in the company. This may involve one or two key senior executives, a whole group of executives, or even a department. The key is that these people have the greatest amount of influence on decisions, operations, and strategic direction.

These six elements helped us to understand what was impacting the current culture, but we also wanted to create a certain culture unique to the merger of GlaxoWellcome and SmithKline Beecham. At the time, we had a saying that we 'wanted to bring the best of both into GSK'. After extensive colleague input at GSK, we wanted to create a winning team that could be nimble, authentic, outward-looking, stimulating and supportive, simple to work in and are proud to work for GSK. We then used the Cultural Web to ask employees what they would want to see and feel across the six elements that would create such a culture. For example, we chose to have no more than three layers of management to make it easy to get things done. Back then, there were a lot of consultants and academics who believed you could not influence culture and you were 'doomed'[31] if you even attempted to try.

Today, there is a general acceptance that you can influence and shape your company culture by the way you lead your company, the reward structures you put in place and the way the organisation is designed and the things you are willing to 'not' accept. So often we allow things to go unnoticed, even though dealing with what is not accepted is a faster route to developing the culture you require. We too often take the rather easier route of saying 'this is what we value' and when someone lives up to that value in their behaviour, we exaggerate the value that behaviour has, whilst allowing lots of other behaviour that is *not* valued to go on without being addressed. For an organisation to influence and shape its culture, it must do both, i.e., state what is valued and recognised and appreciate it when it is exhibited *and* address behaviour that is contradicting the culture you want to build.

Here are some examples of companies going out of their way to create a unique and appealing culture.

Zappos are currently heralded as a culturally aware organisation, so much so that they carry out a cultural fit interview that goes halfway to deciding whether you are a right hire. All hires (even senior leaders) go through a 4-week call centre training, where the 10 core values are instilled into each participant and at the end of the first week, the then Zappos CEO, the late Tony Hsieh, used to pay you $2000 to quit if you decide Zappos is not for you.

Disney is another organisation that takes choices it makes over the people it hires seriously. Using a casting theatre, it openly encourages its new hires to *not join* the cast and only do so if you believe you can provide what Disney requires from you.

Twitter is synonymous with innovation and fun. Every quarter, Twitter run 'hack-weeks', when employees are encouraged to explore their crazy ideas.

Netflix offer 'unlimited days off' and measure an employee's contribution by what they produce, not how many hours they work.

Google, although known for driving the performance of talented 'Googlers', have a place of work that supports their employee's lifestyles with pet-friendly places, gyms and a main campus that rivals a world-class holiday retreat.

Sage has a policy that as a 'colleague of Sage', you can donate 5 days of your employed time every year to work with a non-profit organisation that means a lot to you.

The point is, all these organisations offer something unique and of intrinsic value to its employees that differentiates them from their competitors, such that the brand itself becomes stronger than its competitors. Google has 2 million applications to join every year (5,479 a day!) globally and have set the standard in terms of creating a culture that attracts talent.

The next time you go into your workplace, look for signs and symbols that reflect or jar with your culture. I recently went into a prestigious company that was acquired by another company and on the way to its executive suite, I saw cabinets of memorabilia and awards of work carried out by this company that had been recognised around the world over the last 40 years. I was left wondering why was all this recognition placed in one corridor near the executive suite and not on public display for all employees to see every morning when they come in to work?

Culture is the foundation on which organisational success and personal growth happens. As a leader, if you are driven to create a level of achievement of exceptional performance in your organisation, look first at the culture you have created. Whether you lead the organisation, or a team, you set the tone around performance growth based on the minimum standards that reflect what you are willing to accept.

> What do you accept from others that, going forward, you shouldn't?

Focus on growth and development rather than the management of performance. The generation born between 1981 and 1996, known as 'millennials', already outnumber baby boomers (post-war babies born 1946 to 1964) in the overall workforce today. Multiple studies and surveys show that millennials need regular feedback. They don't want to talk about how things have gone and look back four months or so down the road, they live in a world of immediacy, they want it then and there and they value everyone's opinions (especially their peers), even those that really don't have the position to critique. They love to work in teams and put a high value on the relationships with their peers. This predominant group have come to have a healthy disdain for the old methods of performance management and for these reasons alone, we rightly needed to evaluate the way we review human performance in an organisation.

Now, I must admit, I had my doubts at first when the

movement to axe traditional performance management was gaining momentum. This 'movement' came in over the last 5 to 8 years when the likes of Deloitte and EY moved away from their traditional performance-management processes. As a Management Trainer for Xerox, I had spent years 'training' leaders in the art of 'great performance management' but of recent years, had come to realise that you do not manage performance, you manage people. The reality is, most of what we focus on as leaders, i.e., project management, change management, operations management etc., is all about the management of people. Then the 'big four' consultancies started to write about moving away from the traditional forms of 'performance management'. I suspect you are well acquainted with the traditional performance-management process, it's the one where, once a year, you look back with your leader(s) on what 'went well' but really your leader only wants to focus on the thing(s) that went poorly, so they can make you feel bad about it. Then, to ensure you do not repeat the same mistake again, you are asked to write a development plan, only for the development plan to be put in a file and never looked at again until 12 months later – you remember that process? Well, I was still sceptical. I did, however, begin to see the value of a different conversation and my research into iconic businesses revealed this was already happening. The world in which we do business now is much more forgiving of mistakes; it realises that with the pace of change, the advances in technology and the complexity of doing business globally demands courage, experimentation and collaboration, which often means things don't go to plan and when they don't, we have the opportunity to learn.

We live in a world where a lot of known assumptions are being questioned and as a result, I believe we are not so sure of ourselves as we were 10 to 20 years ago. And rightly so!

The older I become the more I am less sure.

Leadership and in particular, the ability to create exceptional performance requires a learning mindset. Encouraging and utilising learning to gain competitive advantage. As humans, we only truly learn in the moment and if we can do this more effectively, then we are more likely to learn, develop and grow each day.

To learn we must be open to what did not work. Learning by default encourages 'mistakes' and 'failures' and it is these words we shy away from because they are presumed to be negative, but in fact, if we embraced them and used them to extract the value out of the experience, we would be all the more likely to experiment, challenge ourselves and grow. The minute the word 'mistakes' is used in the narrative, people become defensive. In the UK (as I write this passage, the first lockdown is being eased), there are already accusations that the Government is not listening to the scientific advisors and this meant 'mistakes were made'. This type of narrative is dreadfully harmful and could cause more damage in the long run when the next pandemic occurs because it stops us from learning from this one. As scary as it seems, we are learning as we go along with this pandemic and therefore, mistakes are going to be part of the learning process. As a human race, if we are going to thrive in this century and beyond, we must lose the sensationalism that accompanies prominent figures and their 'mistakes' and let them get on with their job and learn.

Hold conversations of value

Bringing this back to business, how do we best ensure our ability to learn becomes a strength of an organisation? We mentioned earlier that for many large organisations that operate globally in complex and highly competitive markets, it is vital the company learns and adapts so that it is continually evolving and strengthening the capabilities it requires to win. Learning is central to this approach. With this in mind, as a leader:

- How valuable are your conversations?
- What impact do you have on others when you converse with them?
- How often do you talk to the people you lead?

In recent commissioned surveys, leaders and the frequency they hold one-to-ones with their direct reports is low. In one survey, only 37% of leaders held one to ones with their employees every month. Now, of course, this does not mean to say that the remaining 63% do not speak to their direct reports at all. I suspect many of these leaders speak to their people and ask the following questions:

- What are you doing currently?
- What's gone wrong?
- Why did it go wrong?
- Who was at fault?

Of course, you get the picture, I am being contentious here, but if you are this type of leader, then ask yourself this, how would you feel if your leader only asked you these questions? What impact would these questions have on your growth?

In leadership development courses I have delivered over the years, I have challenged leaders on this reality and those that accept they only 'see' their people infrequently often respond with, 'we don't have the time' or 'my people don't need much supervision', which I think is just an excuse to not lead. If you are not talking to your people frequently as a leader, *what are you doing*? All too often I see these leaders managing either a load of bureaucracy, or even worse, their own career, by managing upwards, to ensure all things 'look rosy in the garden'. As a leader, your people are the *only* resources that ensure you deliver on your commitments to the business and therefore, you need to lead them well. *Really well*.

> Conversations are part of the work, not additional to the work.

Why do we view 'chatting' as 'not working'? Some people spend all day responding to emails and IMs but dare to chat with another team member and they are viewed as 'not pulling their weight' – what rubbish.

Try developing performance rather than managing it

It is vital you know what your employees need in order to perform well. Understanding is key to effective leadership, and it is all about adopting frequent, short in duration, high-value conversations. This is the key to performance development, personal growth and high performance. Fundamental to effective performance development is the focus on capability and growth. So much of the traditional approach to performance management has been focused on performance not capability. Performance, by definition, is something that has already happened, so talking about something that has already happened and not necessarily gone well and digging into the detail as to 'why' it hasn't gone well, is a futile activity. It is like having surgery without the anaesthetic. Firstly, in these situations, people often reactive negatively to the question, 'why?'. If I asked you 'Why did you do that?', you would have to validate 'why' you did something, so immediately, by asking 'why', you have made the person defensive. It is more useful to ask, 'What did you learn?' or 'What would you do differently next time?'. The assumption here is that they *did* learn something from the experience and are therefore, less likely to repeat the same mistakes and outcomes again.

The only constant is incompetence. All employees have things they need to achieve to better themselves and the organisation. So, when focusing on performance development, it is more relevant and valuable to hone the conversation on what you are enjoying, what's challenging you and how can I (i.e., you, as their leader) help? These are the central questions to a relevant performance development review.

Rid your vocabulary of the question 'How are things going? All you are doing is placing the emphasis on them telling you what is going well, knowing full well that most people (and cultures) don't like blowing their own trumpet for too long, so eventually they will offer up the one thing that didn't go so well. 'Bingo', you now have your agenda for the next hour, an excruciatingly painful autopsy of the thing(s) that went wrong, thus rendering your colleague devoid of any sense of interest, commitment, hope and optimism for the future. Madness really, isn't it?

Let's change the way we hold the conversation on performance with our employees. Use those connection points to lift, challenge and grow our employees so they feel good about themselves, their work and the impact they are having on the achievement of the company goals, as well as the wider impact they are having in society.

Key steps to performance development, regardless of what system you use are as follows:

- Encourage frequent weekly or bi-weekly 30-minute high-value conversations between your leaders and your employees.
- Train your leaders on the value of the 'conversation' and how to hold it, i.e., the art of a valuable conversation that focuses on how they can become 'even better' and what they need from you for the next quarter.
- Appreciate the effort and recognise the outcome.
- Formally recognise and appreciate the 'highs' in terms of the employee's efforts and outputs, explore the things that could go even better next time and prepare together for the next quarter.

- Your role as a leader is to develop your people. Throughout the year, look for opportunities for them to grow their current capabilities through the work they do now.
- Formally conclude with a review of the year and set direction and expectation for the next year ahead.
- Reward what has been achieved but look at overall performance through the lens of the input *and* the output and reward accordingly, i.e., high input but low output could also be viewed as positive performance.

Iconic teams, institutions and businesses look at performance in a more sophisticated way than most businesses. They absolutely set high expectations, but they do not penalise employees if high effort and focus have been given, but for other reasons, the output has not been achieved. How many times have you seen, or been the victim of, working *really* hard *all year round* and achieving some but not all goals, only to be given a mediocre reward/rating and next to no recognition? How motivated are you after that to keep doing everything you can to achieve next year's objectives and targets? It is like the perpetual and often educational 'could do better', which eventually switches most people off.

Don't get me wrong; as a leader, you drive for high standards in yourself and those around you, but as a leader, you should also know where each of your direct reports are in terms of their wider context.

- What's going on for them in and outside of work?
- How happy and engaged are they?
- Do they have the resources to succeed i.e., time, people, budget capabilities, systems etc.?
- What do they love to do?
- What would they love to do *more* of?
- How can you help?

I think this speaks to the heart of the issue with performance management and that is that humans are all too often only recognised for their output. There is often a premium on busyness, activity and delivery with very little time to consider impact, value and whether it delivered the desired results. In too many organisations, humans are treated as machines that can repeat similar tasks efficiently and effectively to a required standard and those humans that don't are deemed 'poor performers'. Humans operate within work and work is part of their wider world that includes the ups and downs of any life: births, deaths, relationships, conditions, illnesses – you get the picture. Great leaders see that picture too. What leaders of iconic businesses recognise is that when their workers come to work, they are carrying all of their life with them, and this affects their motivation, engagement and performance. Put succinctly, know your people.

I remember working with an inspirational inner city educational leader in England who once told me that for approximately 30% of the children who came to his school every day, it was the one place where they felt safe and valued. He went on to tell me that school holidays for him were a time of concern and anxiety because he knew his school was not open and that meant some of his children were now at risk. It started me thinking that just because leaders in business are dealing with adults, *many* adults are still experiencing a level of risk and feeling unsafe and undervalued in their wider world. For the sake of humanity, work should also be a place that not only feels safe but a place that brings out the best in humans, so they feel a sense of growth, of being valued and belonging.

Our ability to learn and grow determines where we are today and where *we will be* tomorrow. As business leaders, we often do not spend time (or at least enough time) to stop and think. In a world that is constantly 'on', it is difficult to step off the hamster wheel, but 'step off it' we must. The level of growth and health for you *and* your organisation depends on it. Take time to think about how you are enabling or disabling the achievement and growth of those that work for and with you.

Great performance is *not always* about winning

I'd like to conclude this chapter with a memory I have that I hope illustrates what we have covered in this chapter and also provides an insight into how my thinking has been shaped over the years. When I was 17, I had been an amateur boxer for 5 years and I loved the sport. I boxed for Reading Amateur Boxing Club and went down to the club to train three nights a week. To say I was keen on boxing was an understatement. What I loved about the sport was the discipline and camaraderie of the team and being part of 'the team' was something I was extremely proud of. I still am. It was a place I felt I belonged. The two coaches there were the late Ron Herbert and Ron Basten. Each had very different characteristics. Ron Herbert was a devout Catholic and family man. He was quiet, humble and a very knowledgeable coach of the sport. Ron had won many national trophies at amateur and then professional level in the light welterweight division and boxed for the British Army at the same time as 'our' Henry Cooper (the first man to knock Muhammad Ali off his feet). Ron was, as was mentioned at his eulogy, one of the 'nicest men you'll ever meet". For me, he was one of the most encouraging coaches I have ever had in my life. He had a knack of making you feel like you were unbeatable and that he had your back. Ron Basten, on the other hand, was for me, a more formidable coach but no less effective. Whatever you did, there was always room for improvement and when you had him in your corner, if you were boxing the wrong fight, in between rounds, you would know about it. When I look back on that period of my life now, I have so much affection and love for them both. They taught a young adult much more than how to box. One of the many lessons I will never forget was in 1981. I was picked to represent a Home Counties boxing team to box in a tournament in Kesh, County Fermanagh, Northern Ireland. I still remember the team talk at Heathrow, when about to board the flight to Belfast. Ron Basten stated, 'I don't want any of you to worry, we have been assured a safe passage.' – into what was then a region of Northern Ireland that was a hotbed of Irish Republican Army (IRA) activity and we were an *English* Boxing team going to a high-profile tournament! To say we were all nervous was an understatement and it wasn't helped when our 'guests' picked us up from Belfast Airport in the local funeral hearse and associated black limousines. When we eventually entered the sports hall where the tournament was being held, the atmosphere was electric and charged with a generally good-natured dislike of the English team that had 'dared' to visit. On the way to the tournament hall, we passed all manner of vehicles, bikes, tractors with carts and coaches, all ferrying the audience to what was going to be a 'good night of fighting'. The Irish have always been known to love a good fight.

When the tournament started, we lost the first six bouts which meant that when I went to the ring, I had to win to keep the team in with a chance of winning the overall contest. My entry into the ring was something I will never forget; essentially a thousand hostile people wanting you to lose. Once in the ring, I remember Ron Basten looking me in the eye and saying amid the noise, 'It's just another bout, you've trained for this and you're ready, go out there and do your best.' Fortunately, I won and so did five of my teammates, meaning the last fight was the decider. We lost that fight and in doing so, the overall contest. In the dressing room, we were all drained and dejected, having lost the contest. What I remember most from that night was Ron Basten coming into the dressing room while we were all sitting there and saying nothing. After a few further minutes of silence, when he had everyone's attention he slowly and deliberately looked at each of us in the eyes and slowly put his thumb up, or down, to express his view on our performance that night. What I learnt that night as an impressionable teenager was that for Ron it was *not* about winning, it was about your performance that night. How you held yourself, your mindset and your fight strategy, your energy, fitness and sheer will to pivot, overcome and win. That night, some who won got a thumbs down, and some that lost and yet had tried their hardest got a thumbs up. At that point, we all knew where we stood and whether we had done well or not, it wasn't about the victory. Ron never said another word that evening.

Businesses place so much importance on the result. It's where the glory is and it's where share price is valued, and yet savvy investors view organisations through the lens of performance and asked the question: is this company doing the right things, in the right way, to the right level, that will determine long-term success? What if you as a leader placed more attention on how someone is doing rather than what they are achieving? How would it differ and what culture would it create?

In summary: questions, provocations and actions to increase growth:

   a. How much are people willing go above and beyond for you or the organisation?
   b. How much are they willing and able to take risks, to fail, learn and grow?
   c. To what degree do you really value the human, or do you only look at the output?
   d. How much pressure is placed on people performing?
   e. What happens to people if they make mistakes?
   f. Where do you focus most - the output (result) or the input (the activity)?
   g. What performance and growth culture are you creating and how valuable are the conversations you are having within it?

Remember:

- Be forensic in how and who you bring into your organisation. Especially at the more senior levels. Make sure you are hiring the right people in terms of cultural fit, as well as capability.
- Look for and study 'positive deviants': they will provide insights on how to help others raise their game.
- Length of experience is not a predictor of capability.
- Look for those with the ability to learn and who hold a growth mindset.
- Focus more on how they are doing, not on what they are achieving, and help them establish habits that develop stronger capability *every day.*
- Remember to appreciate the individual attributes to performance as well as recognising the outputs if you want to motivate people towards higher levels of achievement.
- People learn in the moment, so give feedback in 'real time'.
- Never ask the predictable question of, 'How do you think you have done?' Ask, 'What have you learnt and what would you apply going forward?'
- Capability is the measure of skill, understanding, knowledge and behaviour. A human's capability to perform is also reliant on having: a winning strategy, appropriate targets and goals, relevant data and systems, as well as the efficient processes and available resources. Keep in mind that the reason some may fail is not always because of their capability.
- Feedback is a short conversation, i.e., I saw this, you did this, this is what I expected, ending in a question. Do not focus on personal attributes if your feedback is developmental or negative e.g., you were… 'haphazard', 'lazy', 'incompetent' etc. Focus on what you want.

- Humans are born to thrive and grow. Keep this in mind and limit the amount of control mechanisms systems you put in place that limit creativity and high performance.

Chapter Five: Belonging instead of isolation

You cannot be at your best if you feel like you do not fit in. You will spend more time preoccupied with gaining a sense of belonging, or trying to fit in, than you will performing.

Do you remember your first day at school? I do. Do you remember what it felt like to say 'goodbye' to your parents and walk into your school for the very first time? Perhaps you were excited or just plain scared. I was scared. The chances are that it was for many of us an unnerving experience, especially if you didn't know anyone there. When you walked through those gates, what was going on in your mind? I'd hazard a guess it wasn't, 'I wonder what I am going to learn today'. What was going on for you was probably a lot more primal – survival.

Walking through those gates, the first thing you wanted to do was to make friends and fit in. I still remember my first day when I really didn't know anyone in the school, and I was told where my tutor class was, and the teacher put me next to Nigel. I remember sitting down next to Nigel and saying to him, 'Hi, I'm Steve', to which he replied, 'Hi Steve, I'm Nigel'. I remember feeling that sense of relief that in that short intro he had remembered my name and appeared to be friendly. Suffice to say, for the next 5 years, Nigel and I were the best of friends.

The point of all of this is that to build an iconic company, you need to build a sense of belonging that starts with the first impression a person has when they enter your business.

Could do better

All too often 'onboarding' (sometimes called 'induction), which is the way in which businesses bring in and assimilate their new employees to the organisation, is hit and miss and the reality is that first impressions count.

If we were reviewing the onboarding experience for most new hires in organisations today, I believe we would have to grade it as 'could do better'. The complexity of an organisation and the sheer amount of logistical orchestration to ensure all that a new hire needs when they arrive on their first day is immense. I understand, truly I do, but we must start to place an emphasis on this being a great experience if we are looking to create a strong sense of belonging.

It's basic really, but making sure that your new joiners have their security passes, desk, equipment etc. on their first day and they have a planned itinerary for their first week, month etc. says to them 'you care'; it also says that you have joined an organisation that is efficient and understands the value of doing things right. The most common experience in most organisations I have worked in is that the onboarding is reasonable to inconsistent. We are either too busy or too muddled by what we need to do that we become drained from the whole process and pass it on to someone else to deal with. Many organisations see this as just another process, but to create a sense of belonging is much more than a process and in fact, it starts well before day one. The experience you put candidates through, even in the 'attraction' stage (the stage at which they look up your company and are curious to know more), tells them what it is like to work at your company. Many organisations are always changing their operating model or internal processes or function design to create greater value, less cost etc., without realising that in doing this, it often negatively impacts on the core people processes that make people feel valued and wanted. Every time there is a change, it brings into question who now owns what, and do we now have the resources needed to provide the same level of service or enhance it? I guess at the end of the day, this is business, right? And as leaders, it is down to us to manage and resolve these issues, but let's not make it hard for ourselves, especially where human emotion is concerned. It is true with all humans, if we remember one bad or negative action that didn't make us feel valued or wanted, it brings into question the whole relationship, and we hold on to those emotions for some time. Feeling a sense of belonging to the place you work increases your pride, engagement, your desire to go the 'extra mile' and loyalty to that business in the very early stages of your career. As mentioned before, it is often the small actions that have the biggest impact.

Have your new hires join a cause rather than just a business

One of the most memorable onboarding experiences I have ever had was with GlaxoWellcome. The start date was scheduled so that I started with 20 other newbies and after I had been shown around my office and introduced to a few people, I was ushered into a conference amphitheatre. I took a seat, the lights dimmed and along with the other 20 newbies, we listened to the stirring music of Samuel Barber's Adagio for Strings and were shown an emotive film about disease, humanity's greatest threat. During the 10-minute film, statistics that came up on screen covered how many children die in the world *every minute* due to malnutrition, the death rates of diseases like AIDS ... you get the picture. At the end of the film, which had no spoken words, the stirring music started to subside and the screen produced the text: 'Humanity has no greater threat than disease, disease has no greater threat than GlaxoWellcome', at which point the presenter and host then walked on to the stage and said, 'Welcome to GlaxoWellcome'. I was sold. I hadn't joined an organisation in that moment, I had joined a 'movement'. I wanted in. That first day I could have been shown to my desk and given lots to read, but instead, with my fellow newbies, I joined a cause.

Onboarding is about building an emotional connection to what you have joined.

Joining the Red Arrows

Ever wondered what it was like to join one of the world's greatest military air force display teams? I was once waiting to speak at an international leadership event at the Royal Airforce Force (RAF) base in Duxford, England. Waiting in the wings, I started to speak to a Red Arrows pilot, who was also speaking at the event. He told me how since being a kid, all he had ever wanted to do was fly. He told me how he had studied hard and gained the grades to be accepted into the RAF and flew Tornado GR1 ground attack fighter jets in the first Gulf War. At the end of the Gulf War, he tried out for the Red Arrows, something that had been a dream for him ever since he was a young boy. The Red Arrows are officially known as the Royal Air Force Aerobatic Team. Founded in late 1964, they are arguably one of the best, if not the best, military aerobatic teams in the world. The interesting part of his story was that after going through the rigorous tests to join, he was eventually accepted into the Red Arrows. At that point, he was filled with self-doubt. Here was a confident, highly intelligent, gifted and commemorated RAF pilot sharing with me his feelings of inadequacy, doubt and fear. He went on to tell me that when he arrived at RAF Scampton on his first day, he felt sick with fear and anxiety ('like a first day at school'). But he was joining an iconic organisation. He told me that as he walked down the corridor, there were pictures on the walls of all the RAF pilots who had flown with the Red Arrows since 1964, heroes of his; at this point, all he had wanted to do was turn back, but just before he reached the door to the team room, a picture caught his eye. On the wall next to all his heroes was a picture of himself. He openly told me that as he was looking at the picture of himself, he began to cry with pride and relief – he had arrived. He was where he belonged.

Interestingly, in both these examples, it was the small thoughtful actions that created the greatest sense of belonging i.e., all newbies starting on the same day, a stirring video about why you are in business, a picture on a wall.

> What would it take to put a personalised welcome sign out for your new starters?

I understand it wouldn't be easy for all companies to adopt an approach that has this impact, but at the very least, your new hire needs to feel welcomed and feel like they are joining a place where they will feel safe and valued. Without this sense of belonging, humans naturally feel fearful and when fearful, non-rational feelings stop the brain from functioning at its optimal level because its efforts become more tuned in to surviving.

> You cannot feel you belong if you cannot be yourself

Organisations can be exclusive, but leadership should *always* be inclusive. How much are the employees in your organisation able to be themselves? Or do you place a certain emphasis on certain ways of acting and behaving so they belong to the 'tribe'? What kept us safe circa 10,000 years ago when we were in our tribes, and we first started to herd cattle, was all about making sure that everyone complied with certain rules and fitted in and did not bring the herd into danger by doing something risky. What will ensure your organisation's success in the future is not compliance to certain norms, but to have people in your organisation that recognise what works and challenges that which does not. You will need leaders who can untap the diversity of thought that often lies dormant in most organisations. Diversity of thought that could provide you with a game-changing idea. The work that needs to be done in many organisations is by nature complex and multifaceted, so tapping into the collective diversity across your organisation is vital for future success.

When you meet someone who is being authentic, I often think, just like leadership, it can be felt. Your interaction with them seems 'real' and what is being discussed would be valued as being truthful and accurate, sometimes at the cost of it feeling uncomfortable. Authentic people tend to speak their mind. Do not mix this with being sarcastic, rude or arrogant: authentic people can still be empathetic and thoughtful in the way they put across the message. For authentic people, it is the message that counts, *as well as* how it makes you feel.

Sadly, in far too many organisations, being *you* can be a challenge.

Red shoes

Perhaps the most peculiar and by far the most memorable evidence of authenticity and the impact on a person feeling they belonged was on my first meeting with a senior medical professional who worked for a global pharmaceutical company. I remember my assistant who set up the meeting mentioning this person in the run-up to the meeting and in a whispered breath telling me, 'This person isn't your typical employee'. When I dug into why they were not the 'typical employee', I didn't get an immediate answer until the day of the meeting. As scheduled, I turned up at this person's office and entered; on entering, I noticed immediately that he was wearing bright red shoes; red shoes that were being worn with a smart blue suit. We had the meeting and I remember leaving his office thinking he seemed like a nice guy. I went back to my office, only to be greeted by a few other employees and my assistant who questioned me on what I thought of him. I remember at the time feeling uncomfortable; firstly, about being questioned on my view of him; and then secondly, owning up to the fact that I had noticed his bright red shoes.

For a few months, this played on my mind until it came to the company's annual conference. Since our first meeting, I had met up with and worked with him a few times on leadership, teamworking and researching cultural elements relating to the way his part of the organisation worked. I had enjoyed our interactions immensely, further endorsing my original conclusion that he was, in my view (now) a 'thoroughly nice guy'. On the day of the conference, we were all waiting for the coaches to take us to a hotel in London's Park Lane, and I happened to use the same one as my friend with the red shoes. I asked if I could sit next to him, and on the short journey into central London, got to know him more on a personal level. Turns out he was a Quaker and lived in England, but also had a home in France. He was multilingual and grew up in the former Yugoslavia. We spoke about the Yugoslavian war and the heartbreak it had created. I was so enthralled with our conversation that after the conference, I sought him out again so we could chat on the return trip back to the office. This time he had his legs crossed and, yes, his big bright red patent leather shoes were staring me in the face as we chatted some more. It occurred to me, probably fuelled by the fact that I had had a few glasses of wine and we were getting along so well, that I should ask him, what's with the red shoes? So I did, and I'll *never forget* what he said. 'I wear these shoes because I don't want to be like everyone else'. He went on to say, 'I could wear black or brown and be like them, but I wear red because I want to be me'. I was stunned. He also went on to say that he had been working at the company for coming up four years and no one, until now, had asked him, 'Why red shoes?'

Although iconic organisations create a strong sense of belonging, they also create a strong sense of individuality, a sense that it is safe to be you. Conformity to a particular norm, therefore being less authentic, can, and does, happen daily, and people often don't even realise it. Take dress code as an example. Dress code, as in 'smart casual', has many variations of interpretation. For me, it means not wearing a tie, and, I used to like wearing a tie, to me that is smart and to me wearing a tie makes me feel *more me*, i.e., more authentic. I've lost count of the number of times, when working in' a 'smart casual company' and wearing a tie, I have been asked: 'Going anywhere nice after work?' Or even better, 'How did the interview go?' – due to employees seeing me in a suit and tie. Unknowingly, these comments are in some ways encouraging me to come to work without a tie, so I fit in, and yet in doing so, I become less of me (my tie is my friend's red shoes all over again). We all want to fit in and feel we belong, but not at the expense of turning in to someone we are not and in doing so, become inauthentic. Being someone you are not is draining. Unfortunately, many organisational cultures take on the tribe mentality of 'don't do that - do this' to ensure people fit in; these organisations erode individuality and with it the freedom to express, disrupt, challenge and innovate.

It would seem there are two levels on which authenticity shows up in an organisation. Firstly, *who* you are i.e., what you look like, your background and experiences etc., and I call this the outer face; secondly, *how* you are, i.e., your thoughts, views, expressions and how they come across; I call this the inner face. Leaders in iconic businesses uncover the richness of both levels (outer and inner) and therefore help their employees express themselves daily and thoroughly, regardless of context.

How much do you truly listen?

There is a competitive advantage to creating an 'individualistic tribe' where all forms of humanity can openly express their views and those views are listened to. To think about this from a different perspective, it may be helpful to view organisations as organisms, i.e., living things. In some ways, organisations are living systems and it is the role of the leader to first and foremost make the system as healthy and as functional as it can be. One important aspect of human well-being is that people can express concerns, issues, contrary points of views, and in doing so, are heard and valued. Humans are more likely to 'agree to disagree' if they felt they have been listened to (more on attention in the next chapter).

'We're all individuals'

Leaders need to have a cultural nose for sniffing out inauthentic behaviour and facilitating greater levels of individual expression. Effective collaboration and innovation are all about harvesting the individual views of others in a safe and risk-free environment. Encouraging more levels of authentic interaction in an organisation can be disruptive and may provide information that you may not want to hear, but it could be the information you *need* to hear. If you do not have a level of belonging and organisational authenticity, then the chances are, at some point in the near future, your business will be blindly walking off a cliff. No one view should be viewed as 'the view' just because it has been spoken. A leader needs to be cognisant of who is saying it and seek other views when required.

I think we all can relate to people who are 'the voice' of the team or 'organisation' and gladly express their views freely in the hope that they are heard, which is great, but their views often need to be filtered into a wider selection of other authentic views for the leader to make accurate sense of what is being said. What leaders in iconic businesses seek is the truth. The truth of what is going on so they can do something about it, and the level of authenticity leaders create in the organisation will have a bearing on how much truth they hear every day.

Learn it all v. Know it all

Perhaps the best example of a company that was stuck in this type of culture was Microsoft. If you go back to 2014, Microsoft was in danger of becoming extinct, with its share price levelling for the first time in the company's history. Technology was rapidly adopting the cloud and the functionality of smartphones and smart screens meant that the use of the traditional 'desktop' was being questioned. Interestingly, at this point also, Google and Apple were reporting record market share prices. Steve Ballmer, who had joined Microsoft in 1980, worked his way up to CEO and was in the role from 2000 to 2014. Ballmer was Microsoft 'through and through'. He was a towering man with a personality to match, his conference speeches have become the stuff of legend, but during his time with Microsoft, the actual share price stagnated[32]. Testaments from some of Microsoft's employees attest to Steve being first and foremost a salesperson, not a technologist. It is reported that when Steve took over from Bill Gates, the company took a cultural 'right turn' from being an 'innovation' company to a 'revenue' company. There was a lot of energy focused on fighting the competition and so this led to a lack of focus and energy in relation to Microsoft's own products. This is a great example of output thinking where all that mattered was the result, profit, revenue etc rather than taking the long term view. Steve has been criticised for missing out on capitalising on product advances in the tablet, cloud-based internet services and mobile spaces. You can imagine that in this type of culture, any ideas *had* to drive revenue and destroy the competition; the greater the idea, the more value you were worth to Steve. This type of culture, when you consider Microsoft was famed for its innovation, would lead to innovative ideas in creating value in products and services becoming less of a priority and especially when growth, stagnating the need for that 'perfect idea', became even more important with a higher degree of value place on getting it right, rather than trying, failing and learning. Step forward to 2014 and with new CEO, Satya Nadella there was a different emphasis, one of 'learn it all', rather than when Steve was in the CEO chair and only wanted to 'know it all', i.e., know how to win, how to destroy the competition and how to increase revenue. Innovation is predicated on failure, but during Steve's term, 'failure' was *not* an option. Satya said himself, that prior to him coming on as the CEO, 'Innovation was being replaced by bureaucracy. Teamwork was being replaced by internal politics. We were falling behind.'

Satya set about changing the culture from day one, calling out the fact that he wanted to 'Hit Refresh', – the title of his compelling book on how he changed the culture and fortune of Microsoft, a company with 130,000 employees. Satya credits famed Stanford psychologist, Carol Dweck and her book *Mindset*[33] as the inspiration for his company's culture change. In *Mindset,* Dweck extols the values of cultivating a growth mindset. Citing decades of research, she shows that individuals who believe their talents can be developed through hard work, good strategies, and input from others (i.e., a growth mindset), tend to achieve more than those who believe their talents are innate gifts with finite development potential (i.e., a fixed mindset). 'In [the growth] mindset, the hand you're dealt is just the starting point for development,' explains Dweck in *Mindset.* 'Everyone can change and grow through application and experience.'

With his mantra of not wanting 'know it all's and instead wanting 'learn it all's, Satya tapped back into the very ingredients that made Microsoft the powerhouse it was by allowing mistakes, allowing failure and all of this on the basis of fundamentally encouraging increased levels of authenticity. In doing this, his employees at Microsoft were more able to express views, collaborate and innovate together and in doing so, started to heal the wounds of a fractured organisation, where each function and department was once described as a 'warring faction'.

Creating a sense of belonging, where you feel accepted and that you have joined a cause, is one element of 'being well' as an employee, but you also have to feel like you can be yourself and express your views, so the organisation's leaders need to create a sense of curiosity and exploration around your views, past experiences and what you feel and think the organisation could be doing and how it could be different to improve things in the future.

Never underestimate the power of the leader saying in certain situations, 'I don't know' or 'I was fearful of making mistakes' or 'I don't always do the right thing 'etc., as these statements encourage and make it 'right' that others will feel more able to express their feelings and thoughts in the organisation and when they do, it will mean that you are starting to harvest the collective intelligence of the organisation through feelings of belonging.

Perhaps no one has expressed this more beautifully than Marianne Williamson:

> 'Our deepest fear is not that we are inadequate. Our deepest fear is that we are powerful beyond measure. It is our light, not our darkness that most frightens us. We ask ourselves, 'Who am I to be brilliant, gorgeous, talented, fabulous?' Actually, who are you not to be? You are a child of God. Your playing small does not serve the world. There is nothing enlightened about shrinking so that other people won't feel insecure around you. We are all meant to shine, as children do. We were born to make manifest the glory of God that is within us. It's not just in some of us; it's in everyone. And as we let our own light shine, we unconsciously give other people permission to do the same. As we are liberated from our own fear, our presence automatically liberates others.'

The power is in not knowing

It has been my observation over the years that women seem more likely than men to express a level of vulnerability. I have seen this in the training room, as well as when leading large conferences – women are more likely, it would seem, to hold their hand up and either express a view or ask a question, normally prefaced by, 'I may have this wrong but...'. It just seems to me that I have rarely heard a man preface a question with 'I may have this wrong but...'. I know it is not by any means an in-depth empirical study, just my observations over the years, but what do you think? Are women less concerned about knowing it all and being right than men? Perhaps because of the gender biases that occur in organisations, are women more naturally expected to be vulnerable and so are more open and authentic in their interactions with others? Perhaps it is dangerous to take any position on the classic stereotypes due to the huge variations of how we all show up to work, plus the variations in the cultures of the places we work.

Belonging, exploration, and authenticity are the cornerstones to effective collaboration and having an organisation that can freely express its views enables greater levels of not only collaboration, but also innovation and in today's world, these are two of the essential factors not only in terms of organisational success, but also in the progress of humanity. Humanity is hungry for more global collaboration. The evidence suggests collaboration is key to our survival. The world is still organised into continents, countries, regions, communities and tribes and this narrows our ability to come together and through a larger sense of belonging collaborate and solve our most pressing problems. This is the leadership challenge, it is down to leaders to work across borders and self-imposed boundaries and be more inclusive in the way they lead if we are to improve the plight of humanity in the 21st century.

Great leaders' express levels of vulnerability uncommon in other places of work. In the more mediocre places of work, you cannot afford to be wrong or not know. In these places of work, it is either safer to be quiet, or to make sure your point is the best. In these places of work, this leads to a culture of either political point scoring, where ideas have a currency value and the higher up the organisation, the higher the value, or people do not say anything for fear of bad things happening to them if they are wrong or have spoken out of turn. 'Best that the leaders who are paid to make the decisions make them', is the prevailing thought in these organisations. In these types of organisations, ideas are followed based on who they come from and how many people support them, rather than whether it is a good idea or not. In these organisations, it is all about keeping your head down and not expressing too much of an opinion and following the crowd. The higher up you are in these organisations, the more risk you have to carry of making the wrong decision; the right decisions are a given (because that's why you are paid what you are paid) *but* the wrong decisions stick, they stick with you and the more you make, the more your reputation suffers until eventually you are cast aside to a barren land, where no one asks your opinion at all, leaving the decision making to a vital few and you with a lack of belonging. It may seem like I am exaggerating the point here, but vulnerability is the access key to authenticity. If we cannot be vulnerable and therefore, our true selves in those times that matter as humans, we look to others for clues on how to behave and this can lead to greater issues on a personal, as well as organisational level.

The Erosion of Self

There has been a lot written since Festinger's (1954) original theory of self-esteem and social comparison, and they all conclude with the same findings: the quickest route to an erosion of self-esteem is to compare oneself to another. It would seem an obvious link to make, but if you cannot be yourself in an organisational context, then you may compare and adopt a similar behaviour to another who seems to be fitting in, being heard, and being valued. When coaching others, I have often found that this lurks just below the surface of a person who is struggling within an organisation. Struggling to be heard and to influence others. I often think this is because many organisations create an 'exclusive club'. This is a club where the membership is rejected if you do not look a certain way, like a particular pastime, live in a certain area, drive a certain car, speak in a particular way.

The only people who don't feel imposter syndrome are imposters.

Imposter Syndrome is a well-researched term where overwhelming feelings of inadequacy are prevalent in certain contexts, which can often lead to self-doubt, anxiety and underperformance. This is one of the reasons why creating a sense of belonging, and with-it authenticity, is so important in organisations, because this can happen to any one of us. Remember the first day at school outlined previously and do you remember the feeling you had when you were accepted in the school? It may have been when you made your first friend, or when you said something and others laughed, or when you were invited to sit with others at lunch. And when this happened for you, do you remember how 'free' you felt? The feeling that *I can be myself around here and it's ok* – that's when you know you can be authentic. It seems ludicrous, really, that an organisation would take a decision to hire you and then expect you to be something that you are not, and yet that is what many organisations do. Inviting someone to be themselves, to be authentic, is not only liberating for the individual it can be very potent for the organisation, especially when you are needing more: creativity, collaboration, curiosity, exploration, originality, learning, experimentation – all essential aspects of an iconic organisation.

Let's talk inclusion

In a recent Harvard Business Review article, 40% of people said they feel isolated at work and that this was having a detrimental effect on their mental well-being and productivity [34]. Through coaching, I can clearly remember conversations with clients who did not feel like they fitted into the culture, and when you consider the US alone spends $8bn a year [35] on Diversity and Inclusion, it would seem that the focus is solely on the Diversity element of the equation. As we all know, you can have a diverse workforce and yet it must be inclusive to extract the value of this diversity. Creating a sense of belonging naturally creates a sense of inclusivity.

Belonging is also wider than simply making people feel like they have joined a cause and that they have everything they need on their first day. Belonging is also about inclusion and making sure your company is representative of the demographic it works within.

> Do you see you in your workplace?
>
> If so, how many of you do you see?
>
> Who don't you see?

Quite early on in my career, I remember feeling uncomfortable when working in a multinational headquarters just outside London and in a part of London that was heavily populated by Indian and Pakistani communities and yet there was little to no representation of Indian and Pakistani employees in the offices.

As a white male, there are few places I go in the world where I do not feel like I fit in, but I remember once going to the rural outskirts of Shanghai for a work project and feeling 'very western', to the point of feeling uncomfortable because there was no one else who looked like me. I didn't see another western face for a few days. I also feel, as a white male, woefully unqualified to talk about this element of belonging, other than to say that if business is to truly tackle and overcome the challenges it faces and build products, solutions and services that enhance humanity, then *all* of humanity needs to be represented more equitably in the business world, and that isn't the case right now and certainly not at the more senior levels of business globally. To have an employee base that represents the broad spectrum of humanity is not just good for humanity, it is also good for business.

> How can your business be successful if it is not made up of the broad range of people who represent your customer base?

There is more pressure than ever before on boards and leadership teams to take a long hard look at the levels of representation and diversity in their organisations and this needs to continue if change is going to happen and more opportunities rightfully open up for a wider spectrum of society. My current fear is that this could be another 'business fad' and over time, the pressure eases and we go back to where we were. Here, in the UK, it has taken over 30 years to come to some level of gender equity in senior positions in business, and let's hope it does not take the same amount of time to see other areas of representation at senior levels.

Organisational 'values' - a proxy for weak leadership?

It seems rather peculiar to me that when we hire people, we want them to feel they belong and then as soon as they are through the door, we thrust our vision, our mission, our purpose and our organisational values and behaviours on to them and say, 'this is what we value, and this is how *you* need to operate around here to get things done.' This jars with a sense of belonging.

Why do organisations cling to a set of value statements in the hope that they shape how their employees behave, when all the evidence seems to point towards leaders disregarding them, often in pursuit of profit, *even if* it is at the cost of their company's reputation, or from a political perspective pure 'selfish enjoyment'; think a certain Christmas party in UK Government when the UK Government itself were placing everyone in lockdown?

It was Jim Collins and Jerry Porras in their book *Built to Last,* who stated that many successful companies seem to adopt a set of principles called 'core values'. This was in 1994 and over the ensuing years, many of us had credit card size aide-memoires of company values stuffed in our wallets and purses – I was never sure whether I should keep them. I did just in case someone asked me to recite them, although the temptation was to simply bin them! It has always been a source of discomfort for me and has become increasingly so over the past few years. We all know of organisations that spout the need for openness, integrity and doing the right thing, yet flagrantly submit false accounts, or the organisation that values 'safety' yet knowingly place their people in unsafe workplaces, or they damage the environment they work in.

The truth is, organisations go to great lengths to define values in terms of time and money, but for what reason? What is a set of values trying to do, and if it is about guiding the principal behaviours of an organisation, why do they so often fail?

We know that leaders set the tone from the top of the business. This tone creates the culture of the business. We also know that employees will very quickly call leaders to account who contradict what they spout as values and what they do. Values are also core to us as humans and provide a moral code through which we live our lives, so is it right that when we join a company another set of values are imposed on us?

To explore this in more detail, let us consider what would happen if an organisation didn't have values, because all the collective intelligence seems to suggest that you are 'doomed to fail' if you don't have values stated, yet for most employees, they are viewed as words on a card and not necessarily evident in their leaders' behaviours. If you have a value for example of 'integrity', does that really need stating? Isn't that a general need in business if you are going to prosper, and shouldn't you be firing people who say one thing and do the other? In fact, couldn't you argue the same case for the top seven researched values: boldness, honesty, fairness, trustworthiness, accountability, learning, transparency? Would you work for, or hire a leader who was: timid, dishonest, unfair, untrustworthy, blames other, fails to learn and doesn't clearly communicate?

The other issue with values is that if they are a little less value-based and more behavioural – a common example in today's world would be the value of 'innovation' – what exactly what does that mean? For some, it may mean, 'small improvements add up to giant leaps' and for others it may mean, 'we must be radical and rethink *everything*'. You might be thinking, *but isn't that the point of values?* I suppose to a degree, it is; it is to encourage people to be mindful and act in accordance with the 'values' stated. But what if an employee innovates and it fails, and they are chastised for it, or even worse, no one says 'great attempt' or 'appreciate the effort', what then happens to the value of 'innovation'? Does it become undermined?

I think we expect values to shape the way an organisation or team operates but all the evidence is that because they are so often up for interpretation, compromised, contradicted or simply do not align to another's values, they have become something a business does with little actual value to the business itself.

> For too long, we have been using values as a proxy for weak leadership.

If people are dishonest, untrustworthy or don't do the right thing, we shouldn't need a set of values to address the issue. Leaders should feel able to confront the individual accordingly and in doing so, they act out what is valued in that business.

It was Peter Senge who stated that, 'To create a learning organisation that will survive and prosper over time, people need to feel that their own vision and values are connected to the company's.' And in a world where we place a premium on diversity and inclusion, I think this articulates a truer meaning of values and how they should be used.

In the context of belonging how would you feel if a leader was to state: 'We have not written down our set of values here because we trust you have high moral standards around how you do business, and we will hold each other to account if we don't'. Or 'Welcome, we value you for who you are, go do your best work and if there are hurdles in your way then let us know'. Immediately, you are treating your employees like adults, you have set an expectation that 'we operate with high moral standards', we value 'you' and you have an increased belonging through stating that you trust your employees. *That's leadership*.

The one thing we (employees, shareholders and society) could all benefit from is strong leadership, and I am not using the word 'strong' to denote dogmatic, macho, egocentric, rigid and fixed leadership. Strong leadership is really about stating what is acceptable and what is not and measuring another's performance by that standard and assuming you hire, develop and appoint those leaders who know the basics of right from wrong – if you did this, then there's no reason for values.

Creating a place of belonging

A recent Better Up study[36] surveyed 1,789 full-time U.S. employees across many industries, and then conducted a series of experiments with more than 2,000 live participants to observe and measure the costs of exclusion. They found that where workers feel like they belong, companies reap substantial bottom-line benefits. High belonging was linked to a whopping 56% increase in job performance, a 50% drop in turnover risk, and a 75% reduction in sick days. The survey concluded that for a 10,000-person company, this would result in annual savings of more than $52m. Employees with higher workplace belonging also showed a 167% increase in their employer promoter score (eNPS – their willingness to recommend their company to others).

There are three places in the life of any human that should be a place of safety, a place of belonging and a place that can (if you choose) help you grow and develop into the human you want to be, and those places are: your home, your school and your place of work. The household you are brought up in is down to where the wheel of nature lands, but the school you are educated in and the place you go to work, we, as humanity, collectively set the standards you are exposed to in those places. Over the years, schools have come under increased scrutiny to not only educate their pupils to higher grades, but also provide a level of 'pastoral care' (i.e., emotional, social and spiritual care) to their students. This was on the back of recognising that young children all come from different family backgrounds and this plays into how they show up at school. Developing a school's ability to not only recognise this context, but also deal with it effectively helps enhance the educational process for those children, as well as create a place of education that is perhaps (sadly for some) a relief from their home life. I believe the same pastoral care needs to be offered in organisations and in most iconic organisations today, they do view the people who come to work for them as more than simply an employee number.

In 2017, the then Prime Minister, Theresa May, commissioned an extensive report into mental health in the workplace[37]. The remit of the study was to carry out an independent review into how employers can better support all individuals currently in employment, including those with mental ill health or poor well-being, to remain in, and thrive through work. The 'Thriving at Work' study found some alarming facts:

- There is a large annual cost to employers of between £33 billion and £42 billion (with over half of the cost coming from presenteeism – when individuals are less productive due to poor mental health in work) with additional costs from sickness absence and staff turnover.
- The cost of poor mental health to the Government is between £24 billion and £27 billion. This includes costs in providing benefits, falls in tax revenue and costs to the NHS.
- The cost of poor mental health to the economy as a whole is more than both of those together from lost output, at between £74 billion and £99 billion per year.

To bring yourself to work every day and feel like you belong in a place that values you and brings out your best is a blessing that sadly far too few of us are experiencing. Work does not have to be drudgery: even the most mundane task can be made to feel like you are doing something of meaning and value and as result, you are also being valued. Making this clear to your employees who come to work for you every day helps to create a sense of belonging. Only through high levels of inclusion can we create a place where people are more likely to support and collaborate with others. In recent research [38], both correlational and experimental, it was found that the link between ostracism and aggression could be predicted, so it is hugely important that for the well-being of those that join your organisation, as well as the organisation itself, you create a place where people belong.

Exclusion is bad for business and bad for humanity.

That said, over the years, I have seen many people work in quite isolated ways and when I have asked them how they are doing and how it feels in terms of their work, they seem to say that they find joy in the work they do. For these people, to have a purpose and to apply their capabilities to a task suited to them creates an experience that doesn't feel lonely.

Doing work with *no* meaning, on your own however, can feel lonely and this can impact employee well-being. So, meaning and belonging are important for the well-being and performance of your employees.

In summary: questions, provocations and actions to increase belonging:

Belonging is not only about how you onboard new hires in your organisation, it is also about how you build an emotional sense of belonging to your business and how you create an inclusive work place.

- To what degree do you make people feel they belong where you work?
- To what degree can people be themselves at work?
- Do you see a diverse workforce in the employees you work with and for?
- Collaboration is key to your success and diversity and inclusion are key to effective collaboration.

- How much do you engage your new hires on an emotional level?
- To what extent are the people you lead able to fully express themselves and bring their whole self to work?
- To what extent does your organisation's level of diversity reflect the demographic it operates within?
- What creates belonging at your workplace?

Actions:

- How inclusive are you as a leader? To what extent do you seek alternative opinions from a diverse set of employees or community members who buy your product and or services? Engage with and join a different set of people to yourself.
- Who in your world provides a very different point of view to your own? If you can't think of someone, find someone who can challenge your thinking.
- Design and create an onboarding experience that ensures your new hires feel like they are joining a cause; do it well because it creates a better first impression.
- Ensure new hires are offered the support of an organisational partner/teammate who can be there to answer questions/concerns, as and when required.
- Create a well-being strategy for your employees so they can access support, if and when needed.
- Make it clear that you have a set of principles around how you operate at a leadership level and you trust employees to do the right thing – 'that's why we hired you'.
- Remove your values from the equation.
- Ensure all your leaders are trained in being able to both create a sense of belonging and are able to spot and support a colleague's challenges with well-being, if and when required.

- If, as a leader, you are looking to harvest the collective intelligence of your team or organisation, then role model openness and vulnerability – if you don't know something, say you don't know, it says more about your character than your intelligence.
- Look for easy ways in which your employees can help each other out by sharing learning, as well as sharing the challenges they are facing.
- Encourage people to speak up and express their views and when they do, seek not to counter the view, even if you disagree, simply validate the view and recognise the contribution by thanking them for sharing their views.
- Value the act of courage i.e., the ability to assert a view that may not be popular; this will ensure your organisation develops and grows in a rounded way.
- Ensure your organisation is representative of the whole of humanity in all its wondrous forms so that your organisational team reflects the places and people it will be serving and selling to.

Chapter Seven: Attention instead of being ignored

Attention relates to the human need to be listened to and heard with humility, curiosity and without prejudice.

> We are living in a world where we are constantly distracted.

As humans, we have an innate need to be validated through the attention we give and receive from others. It has been stated that 'the currency of leadership *is* attention'. Where do you focus your attention as a leader? In a world that is constantly *on*, and all too often distracted, I suspect, in the context of work, your attention could be on any number of the following: results, reports, processes, data, systems, presentations, up, down or across the organisation; it could be customers, market dynamics, the financials – the list is endless and probably many of these at the same time.

We stated earlier that the average child receives only 8 mins of time from either parent each day (just under an hour every week), how much of your attention (if it were measured in minutes per day/week) is focused on your employees? How much attention do you give others and so create spaces of time where people are heard and validated?

It was Martin Luther King who stated, 'Riots are the language of the unheard'. Unrest manifests itself in many ways and if you deeply listen to any protesters their *primary need* is to be heard.

It is a mistake in many organisations to look at employee well-being and engagement through the lens of reacting to the data and potentially doing more, i.e., focus groups, action plans, round tables, town hall events etc., when really what you are trying to do is salvage the relationship between the leader and the employee. Engagement is down or mental health of workers is an issue, so creating a strategy for higher engagement and better mental health is a distraction – the question needing to be asked is, what quality of relationship do your leaders have with their employees? Are they being listened to and valued? As leaders are we following through on our promises as an organisation and therefore, building trust?

In a world that never switches off, humans are distracted and constantly ignored to the detriment of not just their own well-being, but the well-being of those around them. It is the most basic need of the human soul, that of being recognised, valued and heard. Nowadays, we are inundated with information. Many of us are constantly trying to keep up on social media and other smartphone applications, feeling like if we are not 'on it', we are not connected to humanity and yet this form of connecting is 'light in nutrition'. It is not feeding the human soul and like many, I believe we are still to uncover the full social and psychological impact of technology like the internet, social media and smart devices on us as humans and society more generally.

Sir Tim Berners-Lee's original hope for the internet was that it would bring us all together and to a degree, it has, as it is certainly easier to connect with others. The issue is that it has created divisions in our society because we, as humans, in a drive for belonging and attention, seek out those like ourselves. In an interview [39] on the 30th anniversary of the World Wide Web in 2019, Sir Tim stated, 'While the web has created opportunity, given marginalised groups a voice and made our daily lives easier, it has also created opportunity for scammers, given a voice to those who spread hatred and made all kinds of crime easier to commit. It's understandable that many people feel afraid and unsure if the web is really a force for good. But given how much the web has changed in the past 30 years, it would be defeatist and unimaginative to assume that the web, at least as we know it, can't be changed for the better in the next 30 years. If we give up on building a better web now, then the web will not have failed us - we will have failed the web.' I am a fan of technology and have seen the amount of good it can bring but I am also very wary of the negative impacts it can have on us as humans, especially if we choose to use it in a way that limits our well-being.

We are wired to connect

As part of the world emerges from long periods of lockdown, I have been heartened by the desire and visceral need of humans to come back together again, whether it be at the local bar/pub or sports stadium or concert venue. The pandemic has proven and reminded us that there is no doubt we are social animals and are designed to connect, and long periods of time without human connection can be harmful to our well-being.

Zoom, Skype and Teams are practical ways in which we connect but the level of attention we provide to others on those platforms is limited. We are more likely to connect emotionally and therefore, provide a higher level of attention if we are physically together. We seemed to recognise this early in the pandemic as many leaders started to schedule in time just to come on to a call and chat about anything but work and so hopefully, replicate those spontaneous office interactions that maintain the attention we have on others but (for me anyway) they were not useful for all, they sometimes felt staged and awkward. The lesson here seems to be you cannot schedule informal and spontaneous connections. Physical proximity is the only way we can do that, and it is important if we want to provide a highly nutritious level of attention. There is an unsaid emotional connection when people travel to see others that says you care enough to go and meet them in person, and this will never be replaced by virtual technology no matter how good the connection is.

After the fall of the Romanian communist government in 1989, I remember reading about the Romanian orphans and their standard of care under Nicolae Ceaușescu's regime. Suffice to say, the conditions they were brought up in were unimaginable, they were often tied to chairs for long periods of time and subjected to regularly 'encouraged' and systematic beatings as a form of healthy discipline. To ward off head lice, heads were shaved, which meant it was difficult to distinguish girl from boy and the nurses would often not get them dressed so they would be left alone for hours sitting in their own urine and faeces with no contact from anyone. Most of what we know today about 'childhood attachment' issues were sadly learnt from studies of the Romanian orphans in the 90s. There was one element of the research that struck me at the time, and it turned my stomach, and that was they found that a lack of human contact had a detrimental effect on the growth of their brains, so much so that it impacted their entire lives, meaning that even when they were in new, loving homes, their brains never fully recovered from the horrors of their previous abuse. A lot of Ceaușescu's orphans never viewed any of the people around them as caring for them, they could never identify with a mother or father for example. They had developed what was later termed an 'institutionalised brain'.

The point of this story is that the need for attention – i.e., to be cared for, listened to and loved – *never* goes away, and if organisations don't listen to and care for their employees, then they are neglecting the fundamental need of a human. If you don't care for your employees, how can you expect them to care for your customers? This need goes hand-in-hand with the human need to have a sense of belonging and a feeling of being valued for who they authentically are.

As John C. Maxwell stated, 'If you don't love 'em, don't lead 'em.'

Attention shows up in many ways in organisations, and we tend to associate the investment of time with providing attention. I often hear leaders lament that they 'do not have the time' to spend with their employees because they have 'too much on'. Too many meetings, work, webinars, too much travel… the list goes on. Too much of other stuff that is far more important than showing another human attention, whilst failing to grasp that you get things done through human interaction. What these leaders fail to recognise is that spending time with the people who work for them *is their job*. Progressing work through your people is a central part of leadership. If you are not doing that, *what are you doing?*

Now I admit that some people need more attention than others. And some, in the eyes of the leader, want the time, but do not actually need it, and others say they don't need the time, but actually *do* need it. Your job as a leader is to determine how much, when and where you need to provide attention. Failing to connect with the people you manage is 'neglect', and this can often lead to performance and engagement issues that can catch you out later.

His name was Frank

My first boss was a guy called Frank Howard. At the tender age of just 16 (a good few years back now), as mentioned before, I worked for Burberry. The same global fashion giant of today, but in those days, they were really known only for one thing: the famous Burberry trench coat, a quality coat that had its origins from the First World War (hence 'trench'). Frank was a tiny man with big rimmed glasses that made him look a bit like Mr Magoo. He had been an RAF engineer during the Second World War, working on Spitfires and Hurricanes and as he entered the final years of his working life, he ran the Clothing Technology team. It was a very small team of 3 (of which I was one), who serviced, maintained and repaired over 200 sewing machines, numerous presses and other clothing technology that was used by the 356 wonderful staff that made hundreds of these world-renowned coats daily.

I was a young and rather nervous apprentice, and every day, Frank would ask me how I was doing. When I was stuck on a call (usually a sewing machine that had a missing stitch) and I was struggling to fix the problem, he would never be too far away. He had a knack of coming over (usually asking if I wanted a tea) at just the time I was about to give in, and he'd ask me, 'So, what's going on?' and, 'What have you tried so far?' I'd talk it through with him (normally over the cup of tea) and he'd usually interject at certain points with, 'That was a good idea' or another confidence boosting statement such as, 'I would have done that too'. The thing about Frank was he'd never tell me the answer. The nearest he ever got to it was, 'I am wondering what would happen if...' or, 'You may want to consider...'

Frank was attentive and everything I think a good leader should be. He supported me and challenged me, but most of all, he cared about me. As a result of the attention Frank showed me, I still fondly remember his name 40 years on and when I recall his name, I can still remember how he made me feel: safe, developed and valued.

> How many of the people you have led in the past will remember your name fondly in the winter years of their lives?

Being an 'attention seeker' is no bad thing

We are brought up to believe that 'attention seeking' is a negative. This can lead to people 'playing strong', i.e., needing help, but finding it difficult to ask for it.

Organisations where people thrive listen to each other. Leaders in iconic organisations listen with their eyes just as much as their ears. Giving their employees attention creates greater understanding, empathy and along with higher levels of engagement, helps to build trust. What it also does is it creates a greater knowledge of what is going on. Leaders need to pay attention to what is being said (by themselves and others), but also what is not being said.

Let's be clear, paying attention comes in many guises and if this sounds like the 'soft pink and fluffy stuff', then you may want to evaluate how effective you and your leaders are at the following:

- truly listening without forming responses in your head while supposedly listening
- being brave enough to openly share when you have made a mistake
- recognising and appreciating great work and effort
- addressing poor performance by providing timely, constructive and honest feedback
- being patient enough to spend time with others, without wishing to be somewhere else
- caring enough to remember your employees are humans, not machines, and give them time off when appropriate

If humans in organisations were treated as machines, at the very least, wouldn't they receive regular maintenance to ensure they were not going to break at any point? So, why is it we do not train leaders to do the same with the employees who work for them? If the attention of a business is focused on something other than the employees that work for the business, then this indicates a 'lack of leadership'. This is likely contributing to the general lack of well-being in the organisation. We can no longer assume the people who come to work for us have come from an environment where they feel they belong and where they can express themselves and are fundamentally cared for. Coming into a workplace and working for someone who looks out for them might be the first time they have experienced that in their life. Iconic organisations train leaders to lead the human first (not the business) because they recognise that not only is it valuable for the human, but it is also ultimately valuable for their business results and the reputation of their company.

There are numerous research studies that have investigated the impact of being ignored, or, as it is commonly known, 'being given the silent treatment'. I have witnessed first-hand the impact of others being ignored and there seems to be two responses that humans provide initially, and they are dependent on their level of self-esteem and self-confidence. The first response is 'I'll just carry on because I am sure that if I weren't doing things right, they would tell me'. The second response is 'I wonder if I am doing ok because I haven't had any feedback to say that I am, so I am not sure if I am working to the required standards.' Without necessarily knowing it, the leader who should be attentive to this person is being quite pernicious in their behaviour. This lack of attention erodes self-confidence, so much so that if the leader had any 'doubts' about their capability, they'll very shortly start to see evidence to back that 'doubt' up. Employees who go without attention end up wondering how they are doing. They start to underperform because they begin to overthink everything and instead of acting quickly on things, work starts to slow down, hesitation and self-doubt creep in and mistakes are made. Therefore attention through leadership and feedback are *so important* to the health and performance of the humans that work within the organisation. You cannot have low confidence and still perform to high levels; if you do, it will very soon lead to fatigue and breakdown. Equally, you cannot be emotionally charged with feelings of distress through being ignored and operate in a rational manner.

> As a leader you cannot not communicate. Even if you are saying nothing, you are saying something.

Being ignored can cause emotional trauma or stress. It can lead to loneliness and despair and anger. As stated at the beginning of this book, all the problems we face in this world come down to leadership, and never before in the history of the humanity have we needed leadership to be focused more on the human. Too many leaders have the MBA, the intellect and sheer political savvy to perform well in post, whether that be in public or private office, but fail to place their attention on the human. We need more leaders who think systemically about the impact their organisation is having on the people who work for them and world in which they operate.

> The attention you provide is either building the human or dismantling the human.

Listen with your eyes

What is good for humans is also good for business. Building organisations that listen to their employees is more likely to create a culture where engagement is high, and performance is exceptional. In case you need convincing, try finding a successful organisation where the humans working for it begrudge being there. If people are listened to and validated, it leads to higher levels of engagement because they feel that by being listened to they can influence the way their organisation operates. They become more invested and committed to the cause. Too many of us listen to either judge a person's idea, or we listen to prove ourselves right. The only thing we are listening for is a gap so we can put our own point of view across. Given that approximately 57% of how we communicate *is non-verbal*, when we listen with our eyes as well as our ears, we see what is really going on for that individual. Developing this level of attention in leaders is a powerful way in which leaders can engage with their employees.

When you are attentive as a leader and you see something that seems 'off' or incongruent with what someone says and how they say it, then take time, delve a little deeper. Ask questions that open the conversation rather than close it down. How many times have you asked someone how they are doing and they have responded with, 'Ok, I guess', and you have skated on past with a 'good, great' or 'excellent' as a response, knowing deep down in your gut there is more to the response and you need to explore it with them, but you have too much to do, too many meetings to attend, other priorities and too little time?

The watch-out for all of us is we carry bias that affects where and how we place attention. It stops us from hearing what the human in front of us has to offer, as well as limits our business growth.

It's just a bag!

The most vivid and memorable experience I have had of working with a leader with a very obvious 'bias', and whose attention was distracted, came when we were hiring staff for a new European Contact Centre in London. The hiring leader and I had gained sign-off to hire 8 team leaders who would work for this leader in the European Contact Centre. At the time I had been close to the project in terms of the organisational design and required culture set-up for the centre itself. Working alongside Boston Consulting Group, we had identified the core organisational design and the centre was due to go live in the coming months and with the hiring of the senior leaders, it was now time to hire the team leaders who would effectively manage the circa 90 people who would work in the centre itself. This was a critical layer of leadership, so we had to make sure we hired the right level of capability to ensure the performance of the centre.

For three weeks straight, one day of every week was dedicated to hiring, where this leader, myself and an HR Business Partner would interview candidates.

As I suspect many of you reading this can attest, interviews and interviewees can all merge into one if you are not careful, so it is important that you make notes and do not take too long to compare notes with your hiring partner. I can remember thinking the recruiter had done a good job of screening as the candidates coming through were of high quality. On the second day of interviewing, we had interviewed around 8 candidates and had come together to compare notes at the end of the day. Going through the notes, there was one candidate who we had a difference of opinion on. We discussed and explored the differences, and it became quite apparent my fellow recruiter (the hiring leader at this time) did not want this candidate, who I thought was a strong contender for the role. All explanations were dismissed because she 'clearly wasn't an appropriate candidate to put through to the next round'. I couldn't understand why. For me, this person had answered all the questions well by providing strong evidence that she had the capabilities to do the role *and* do it well. After quite some time going round in circles, I asked the question, 'What was it you didn't like about the candidate?', to which my fellow recruiter responded, 'No one comes to an interview carrying a plastic bag'. I was stunned. Failing to pay attention to what the interviewee had said, my fellow recruiter had made a decision on this particular candidate based on the fact that she was carrying a plastic shopping bag into an interview for a job. Now there are numerous reasons why she may have carried the bag into the interview, but the point is, the bag triggered a bias in my fellow interviewer and shifted his attention. The bag had no bearing on whether this candidate could do the role and yet it put this hiring leader off hiring that person.

It's very easy to read that example and conclude that not

enough attention was given to the candidate and had that hiring leader really listened to the candidate, their minds would have changed, but all the evidence would seem to suggest that when a bias is triggered, listening to and being attentive for information to challenge and perhaps change that bias is not going to happen.

Bias (as stated earlier) informs how we make sense of the world. From the paper someone is reading, to the colour of the shoes they are wearing (as we know from earlier), to the car they are driving; we *all* make judgements on people based on triggers that unconsciously help our brain form an opinion. It saves us thinking! Let's face it, if we did not have our brain working out things for us unconsciously, we would fall over with the sheer amount of information we would have to process. The problem is that these biases can be inappropriate in certain settings, or just socially 'wrong' per se. As a leader, being attentive to your own thinking and way of behaving helps you examine more forensically how you see the world. In doing this, you also start to evaluate the thought itself and ask the question, does it work for you, or not? Doing this regularly as a leader is vital in ensuring your thinking is current and progressive.

> You see the world, not how it is but how you are. – Stephen R. Covey

A word on collaboration. I have often thought that to hire individuals and then focus simply on having them work effectively in a team is not enough. Leaders need to be thinking about how their teams work collectively in the context of the organisation and given (as we stated earlier) organisations are not necessarily easy to navigate and get things done, couple that with the complexity of a business strategy, a matrixed organisation and more than likely not, not enough people to do the work required, then you have a perfect storm that will wreak havoc and lead to business failure.

Collaboration is the art of working together on a common purpose and in my experience, few teams and organisations do this well. As stated earlier, organisations are by nature messy. Normally they have competing agendas and rewards systems in place that cause them to trip over themselves. We have all heard the of the friction between Service and Sales, Marketing and Sales, P&L and Group, Corporate and Function, or Finance, Legal, HR and the rest of the business. Healthy tension, where we must trade off each other to work through and resolve an issue is appropriate but having competing reward structures or incentive plans will create entrenched views and therefore, be damaging to the overall health and wealth of the organisation.

> 'I think it is in collaboration that the nature of art is revealed,' – Steve Lacy

For many iconic businesses, one of the defining elements of the business is that they focus very little attention on the competition, and they do this because their attention is placed on making themselves excellent. They focus a lot of their attention on how to operate efficiently internally. They do this because they recognise that making it easy to work and execute things within their organisation is central to collaboration and ultimate success.

I think this is also where sports analogies and business differ. Over the years, I have had many successful sports stars talk at conferences where the main thrust of their presentation is in the extreme lengths, they (and their team) go to increase performance. These teams and individuals have a forensic approach to attention by looking at how they can be better, and they apply and practice these daily. Many, if not most organisations do not apply that level of attention to performance and so for many, mediocrity awaits.

Collaboration – a winning advantage

Being attentive to each other within a group increases the chances of collaboration and innovation. The mistake we often make is we believe that just using the verb 'collaboration' is enough to make it happen. That is not the case. Collaboration is not a 'factor' of organisational life, it is *actually* a capability, and it is a capability that runs counter to many organisational cultures.

The art of developing collaboration is to define the capabilities needed to create it and put reward structures in that value the act of collaboration. Having observed, worked in and with numerous teams over the years, the capabilities of the leader needed to create collaboration are in fact the same capabilities needed to create high performance and are in fact the four needs of humans outlined in this book:

- **Meaning** - create a clear, common and compelling purpose to be together
- **Growth** - enrol the right people with the right capabilities and trust them to do what is required
- **Belonging** - have a diverse representation of people to enrich the discussion and views
- **Attention** - be inclusive and listen to all views and you are more likely to think outside the box

Another perspective

At the heart of attention is empathy. The ability to be able to view another person's perspective; to be able to feel, think and experience the world from another person's perspective can be *very* powerful. It creates bonds and relationships that build trust and more effective ways of working and long-lasting relationships.

I remember one of the most powerful 'development'

experiences I was ever exposed to was simply a round table discussion. A group of 10 leaders (myself being one of them) was given a common scenario. The scenario was 'a colleague you were managing has started to turn up late for work, you (as their leader) have talked to them about it, they have simply apologised, stating it wouldn't happen again and have continued turning up late for work'. If you are a leader this might well be an issue you have had to deal with. I am also guessing you already know the next step, possibly another conversation, leading to a first formal warning for being constantly late. Well, that was going to be my approach. From where I came from in the business, that was how we would deal with it. But as I listened to all my other trainee leaders talk about what they were thinking and what therefore, they were proposing to do to address the issue, I suddenly realised how narrow-minded I had been, not to mention how unsympathetic and uncaring I would have been if I had carried out my approach based on the information to hand. My fellow trainees approached it from the basis of asking open questions, being curious as to why it was happening, exploring together and collaborating on potential solutions to the problem. I remember feeling so inadequate and narrow in my approach and to this day, I have never forgotten the learning from this.

Empathy (Emotional Quotient, or EQ) can be taught. It refers to the way our brains are formed and the neural networks within them that are set up to understand and perceive other humans' thoughts and feelings. They are stronger in women than they are in men. Numerous studies have found that females have more empathy than men. Women are better at taking other people's perspective and when seeing some level of pain or discomfort, are more compassionate than men in their responses [40]. Being empathetic as humans enables us to live in close proximity to each other without wanting to fight and argue all the time. Empathy is learnt as a child through either seeing others express it, or we receive it ourselves, and when we receive empathy, we recognise the value of it and so are more likely to reciprocate and express it to others. When was the last time you searched out a colleague in your team or organisation who you thought may be struggling and sat down and listened to his or her view of their work? Try this out: think of a colleague and connect with them to see how they are doing. Be open, encouraging and listen to what they have to say. What assumptions had you made about them and which of those assumptions were true, and which weren't? The power of empathy is that your assumptions will become more accurate as you practise empathy with others, and this will build greater levels of trust, engagement and discretionary effort.

Attention is about being curious about the people you have around you. These could be employees as well as customers and other key stakeholders. Giving attention as a leader not only validates them, it also ensures you are connected to the organisation. Leaders who lose this ability to tap into their organisations lose the ability to create iconic places of work and this can lead to creating toxic cultures where fear, anxiety, apathy and disengagement become the norm. Herb Kelleher, the late maverick leader of Southwest Airlines, once stated that, 'A company is stronger if it is bound by love rather than by fear.'

Truly listening to others is, in some ways, an act of love.

Applying this level of attention to those you lead will create stronger relationships and build higher levels of understanding as to what makes the people you lead tick and ultimately will lead to higher commitment and engagement, meaning you may be a leader whose name they never forget in the future because, like my first boss Frank, you made them feel safe, developed and valued as a fellow human.

In summary: questions, provocations and actions to increase attention:

Attention is the currency of leadership. As a leader, where do you focus most of your attention? If it is not on your people and your customers, then your lifespan as an organisation is ticking down and your 'out of business' date' – is fast approaching.

- How much do you really listen to anyone?
- Who do you spend most of your time with and why?
- How much do you encourage and value social interaction at work?
- How often do you have one to one's with your people?
- How interested are you in the lives of the people who work for you?
- What would occur if you spent more time with people listening to what is going on for them?

Actions:

Agree a regular 'one-to-one' schedule for all your direct reports and ringfence the time. At the meeting, be present and make notes of what has been heard, said and actioned, and play it back, i.e.: summarise it at the end of the meeting. If you take an action, then follow through with that action. That says, 'you not only heard me, but you value me enough to action what you've heard'.

Be consistent with where and with who you focus your attention. The worst thing you can do is spend more time with some rather than with others, as that can be inferred as favouritism.

Write down the names of five people you spend the most time with at work. How diverse are their thoughts to you? How much are they challenging and improving your leadership?

Where and when it is relevant to do so, share what is going on for you. This also signals a level of disclosure that establishes trust and openness between each other that often leads to higher levels of attention.

Recognise what the other person needs and work to meet those needs as much as possible.

Grow your levels of empathy by becoming curious as to what is going on for others. Don't be constrained by the amount of time you have with them; be conscious of the amount of attention you pay whilst in their company.

Identify what don't you know, seek out and be open to others views before making up your own mind?

Chapter Eight: A new Leadership Manifesto

At the beginning of this book, we put forward a purpose for work and stated that we should not simply judge the success of a business on share value, revenue, margin, profit or how efficient or effective it was, we should also view a business by how much it supports the growth of the societies and communities it works within and how conducive the place of work is to the human spirit.

The purpose of work is to **do great**, **do good** and **be well**.

We then shifted our focus on to leadership. If businesses needed to balance their attention across doing great, doing good and being well, then what did this mean for leadership? We then stated that leaders need to be trained to focus on the 'human needs'. Meeting the human needs help to create iconic businesses that thrive and proposer and add value to humanity.

The four human needs are :

- **Meaning** – have a purpose for being in business that is clear and compelling and that creates a cause greater than simply profit..
- **Growth** – create an environment where people are trusted to do the right thing and have the freedom to grow and thrive.
- **Belonging** – create a place where people feel they can be themselves, where they are safe to express themselves and their full potential.
- **Attention** – create space for people to be heard and validated as humans, where people are curious to know what they don't know and find innovative ideas to overcome business challenges.

Ever been part of the stampede?

I often think that there are two ways to define whether your organisation is healthy or not. The first is how many times your employees smack the snooze button every morning and the second is how quickly they leave the building when it is time to go home. I remember once standing in an office, where there was over a thousand customer contact staff, and suddenly hearing a rumble. If you have ever seen the film *Jumanji,* it was the sound that the herd of elephants and buffalo make when they are on the move at pace. I distinctly remember thinking, '*What was that?*' The whole building was shaking. I thought we were experiencing an earthquake in England. I was so concerned I asked a colleague, who nonchalantly responded, 'It's 5 o'clock, people are going home.' A few weeks later, I was speaking to the Chief People Officer and relating this experience with some level of surprise that a thousand people would all leave, all at the same time, only to block up the car park for 45 minutes, to which she replied 'There's nothing wrong with that, we do not want to encourage presenteeism.' I was astounded. I agree, we *do not* want to encourage presenteeism, but the fact that everyone spent the last 10 minutes of the day preparing for a mad rush to their cars to get out of the place only to sit in a traffic jam, was for me a sign that things were not healthy in the organisation. Too many of us do work, or work for organisations that we can't wait to get out of – why? What's the mental wellbeing implications of being somewhere where you spend all your time there wishing you were somewhere else? If they had better leadership, would they feel more inclined to stay a few minutes longer, take pride in finishing the last call, or customer query and closing down after a productive day that is recognised by their leader.

We deserve better

I believe we should look at leadership in the same way we

do 'fresh water' – just as all humans on this planet need and deserve fresh water, they also need and deserve great leadership. In fact, I would go so far as to say that the *only way all humans* are ever going to have access to fresh water is through great leadership. The problems our world faces today cannot be solved through the thinking that has brought us here. For far too long, we have developed leaders to be mainly left- brain, logical and detached thinkers, whose sole purpose is to create share value and efficiencies *at any cost*. These leaders (political or organisational) have been measured and rewarded by time-honoured metrics that indicate economic or organisational growth, not by the impact they are having in the world in which they live. This needs to change. 'Kill or be-killed' as a business dictum needs to be consigned to the past. 'Win inclusively and we all win' should be our new mantra. Use competition to enhance your own impact on the products, services, customers and societies you serve. We need businesses to shine brighter than their competition and outdo each other through constructive collaboration and more humanity-led activities and measures.

How can we honestly talk about an 'inclusive' organisation, or society for that matter, if the organisation is not doing its bit to represent the world in which it lives? You can, if you like, file this manifesto in the 'too utopian', or 'the soft pink and fluffy box' and go on your merry way; however if I may, a word of caution! History is littered with great examples where the few have not listened to the many. And the many are beginning to cry out for a different world of work. As we come through this pandemic, it offers us an opportunity to rethink the purpose of work.

We stated earlier that the biggest challenge facing businesses generally is this erosion of trust and it's true, but businesses, according to The Edelman Trust Barometer[41], are still more trusted than NGOs, Government and the media, but we in business cannot be complacent. I believe if we do not address this need for greater leadership now, as the world becomes even more fragmented, unequal and it faces more global crises like disease, financial crashes and environmental disasters, *more and more* people will become displaced and disturbed by what they see and experience and this could lead to a global back lash. By that I mean a state of severe unrest, where the many come together to challenge the few. If we do not begin to change now, humanity will surely face increased disruption in the future.

Bored with the conversation

Over the years I have read many books and attended numerous webinars on leadership and what it means, and I am bored with what I read and the conversation we are having on the topic. I am bored with it because it all too often focuses on the leader and how they need to 'be' to benefit the business they work for. That for me is way too narrow. COVID and recent events in Politics and Eastern Europe have taught us that humanity relies on leadership more broadly and without leadership centred on our human needs, we will be destined for more unrest and misery and ultimately, we will fail humanity.

The leaders we desperately need in today's world are ones that are:

- curious to gain perspectives from people *different* to them.
- able to create meaning and a sense of personal value for humans through the work they do and the businesses they create.
- socially conscious and look for building wider 'gains' between business and the societies and communities they work within.
- constantly learning and challenging themselves.

- comfortable with being wrong, failing and learning.
- skilled at taking a short-term *and* long-term view.
- humble and can park their ego.
- recognise the value of the human as the centre to their business and care for them accordingly.
- able to balance 'doing' with 'viewing' the impact they are having on their business, their employees and customers and the broader society.

We need to rewrite the role of leadership for this coming century and establish a standard of leadership that is right for the evolution of us as humans. No longer should we differentiate the role of the manager and the leader. They are two sides to the same coin. More can be done and more should be done to help those leaders who come to the fore in this pivotal period in our history, to see business through the world and through different perspectives. We need leaders who are inclusive, empathetic, creative and driven to make a positive change in the world by building an iconic business. This focus will be *the* competitive advantage, so that customers and employees alike who come to work for and buy from those organisations feel they are investing their time and money into a business that is meaningful. It is not one or the other (i.e., do great *and not* do good), it is *both,* and we need to lobby governments and business schools and organisations so they too can see the value of the 'virtuous interdependencies' between creating a great organisation that does good *and* is a place where humans thrive. This will be what it means to be successful in business in the future.

A brighter future

In the first quarter of the 21st century, we have seen the very best and the very worst of leadership. For me, this has confirmed the view that leadership and the ability to rally people for the good of humanity is something the world needs more now than ever before. We cannot continue to appoint leaders into positions of influence who only have their own self-interest at heart; yes, it makes for compelling reality TV when we watch the news on how the political leaders of today are doing and how absurd they are being in a seemingly senseless race to gain likes, ratings and followers, but in *reality,* it is damaging our societies and our wider world.

The obvious question is, how do we ensure we appoint and develop these leaders? This is not an easy question to answer. On the political front, democracy is the way in which we (the people) vote for our leaders. The world's democracy index [42] rates country regimes under the following headings: Full Democracies, Flawed Democracies, Hybrid Regimes and finally, Authoritarian Regimes. Interestingly, and rather alarmingly, only 4.5% of the world's population live in a Full Democracy (only 20 of the world's 167 countries). Even the United States was downgraded to a 'flawed democracy', stating a myriad of reasons dating back to the 1960s. This leaves 95.5% of the world's population living in a democracy that is either flawed or in outright authoritarian leadership regimes. In the political field, there should be no part for leadership that only seeks to extend its own interests. The interest of political leaders has to be for the benefit of all, not just the few but this is the same for all leaders – remember our definition of a leader is someone who has the welfare of others at its core. The more the gap between those that have and those that have not widens, the more fragile our existence on this planet will become; and eventually, all the problems we will have to overcome will come down to leadership and whether we have the 'leadership' we need to overcome them.

In leadership *we must begin to trust.*

In the commercial private sector, the accountability for the appointment of leaders often comes down to the board (this is largely dependent on the level of guidance and support the board provides). On a more positive note, in the world's democracies, more board members and shareholders are being vocal if they see wrongdoing in the businesses they back.

For example, a shareholder of Oracle[43] is suing the IT giant for little to no progress in creating racial diversity in its workplace. Qualcomm[44] in the US has also suffered the same issue. This has led, rightly, to many US brands rethinking and re-evaluating the diversity of its company and no doubt spurred on by the inequalities raised by the Black Lives Matter movements, these will continue to redress a wrong in today's society. These are positive examples where either an individual shareholder or a board have created the appropriate pressure on the business to do the right thing. Indeed the 'calling' from this book is to inspire more employees, customers, shareholders, leaders and boards to look more closely at the activity of their businesses and the way they are being led.

Here in the UK, the Corporate Governance Code[45] (referred to as 'the code') was established in 1992 after the Bank of Credit and Commerce International (BCCI) and the Robert Maxwell scandals broke. Robert Maxwell was a billionaire business mogul who, when he died in 1991, had left a £460m hole in the pension funds of his companies. At that time, 'the code' was quite rudimentary, i.e., the CEO and Chair of companies should be separated; boards should have at least three non-executive directors, two of whom should have no financial or personal ties to executives; and each board should have an audit committee composed of non-executive directors[46]. At the time, these quite basic recommendations were viewed as highly controversial. Today, 'the code' is part of UK Company Law and is overseen by the Financial Reporting Council. 'The code' sets out what good corporate governance is for all FTSE listed (London Stock Exchange) companies and applies the right levels of pressure in relation to such areas of governance as executive renumeration, leadership and the relationships with shareholders – all the fundamental areas of governance that, if left unchecked, opens businesses up to potential malpractice and abuse of power. Interestingly, since the Corporate Governance Code's inception in 1992, 90 other markets (jurisdictions) have either started to develop their own version or explained corporate governance codes, but the United States has not.

In 2015, David Ulrich wrote a book called *The Leadership Capital Index*, in which he stated that when it comes to evaluating a company, leadership *really matters*. Many investors look at companies through the lens of strategy, brand, products and services, along with the markets that these organisations are operating within, and yet all of these decisions from strategy to brand, from business development through to business execution, come down to leadership, and of course the quality of these decisions matter. Investors are beginning to be interested not just in the credibility but the capability of the leaders they choose to back. Investors are becoming more curious in terms of how the company is being run and the impact it is having on its people and society more widely. There is an increasing recognition that having a good business idea without the leadership capabilities to fully extract the value of the idea renders the idea impotent. In the book, Ulrich outlines 10 Leadership Index factors; 5 relating to the 'Individual Level' and 5 relating to 'Organisational Level'. The Leadership Index, in many ways, articulates how leaders should lead in broad compliance to 'good governance' as it relates to 'ethical leadership' behaviour, 'strategic execution' and 'taking employee motivation' into account when increasing the pace at which things are done.

The tide has turned

With regards to businesses becoming more accountable for the way they conduct business, we are moving in the right direction. As we covered earlier, the attention ESG (Environmental, Social, and Governance) is rightfully receiving is ensuring the appropriate focus and balance is being placed on creating more ethical businesses, but this requires a different leadership emphasis. As we all know, most change isn't a reaction to something overnight and the changes in how we view work will not happen overnight either, but changes *are* happening.

For many, the COVID pandemic is yet another warning that if we do not collaborate and heal the world's most basic issues, then we will surely be caught out again. Financial crashes, economic hardship, environmental challenges, political posturing/division and global health issues will continue to be leadership's biggest challenges in the future, meaning more needs to be done to create leadership that is fit for humanity.

Rather than send leaders off to lavish hotels for development, where they are wooed by the enormous intelligence of the lecturers and trainers who 'speak at them' about a topic they are familiar with, I think it is more valuable to place development in the communities in which the organisation lives and breathes. Exposing your leaders to lives different to their own helps build humility, empathy and leads to a more inclusive awareness of what humanity is experiencing.

I propose a global standard for leadership that defines leadership clearly for *all* businesses. This isn't about forming a leadership cadre that looks like they are all carved from the same rock, it is about setting a minimum standard of what we should expect of leaders. If doctors take the Hippocratic oath to 'do no harm', so should leaders.

The Leaders' Oath:

As a leader I commit to doing no harm to the institutions and people I lead and the societies and communities I serve. I will lead with a focus on the human. I will create products and or services that will enhance and positively progress the lives of humans and that will do no harm to humanity. As a leader, my business, once profitable, will commit to giving back to the societies and communities it serves, either with a% of profit, or time my employees can dedicate to helping a charity of their choice in work time. I commit to investing in my people just as much as my products and services and recognise that it is the investment in my people that will secure the future success of my team and business. I understand that being a leader will, at times, mean I have to make tough choices, and, in those times, I may have to make people redundant and, in those instances, I commit to doing everything to ensure my employees are not cast aside and that they are supported in finding alternative employment.

If the human is the most valuable asset, then let's treat 'it' as such. I have visited many business schools over the years, both here in the UK and the US, and have been impressed with the level of research and thought that goes into such topics as: Corporate Affairs, Cyber Future, Strategy Planning, Future proofing scenarios, Business Finance, Innovation, Customer Centricity, Strategic Leadership to mention a few; however, the human in the system of work seems to be a conversation we are not having and yet need to. Business schools are a valid forum through which these conversations should be facilitated. If we have such topics as Strategic Leadership why not Human Centred Leadership. It could focus on the psychology of human needs outlined in this book and how they impact performance and the development could take place in parts of the world that need community support while developing leaders. The Green Door Project and Emerging World do great leadership development programmes in this space.

As stated on JUST Capital's website[47], the U.S. private sector alone is worth $19 trillion, which is four times the size of government and 40 times the size of philanthropy. With these numbers, you can quickly gain a sense of scale as to the 'good' that could be done if businesses gained more value by the way they grow trust through their social advocacy. Since 2015, JUST Capital has surveyed more than 96,000 Americans on what they believe U.S. companies should prioritise when it comes to 'just' business behaviour. The people's priorities in 2019 was first, 'pay a fair wage' and the last was, 'generate returns for investors'. It seems a little ironic now to suggest that companies in the future who 'do good' by simply 'paying their employees a fair wage' will receive a higher investment score and so be valued more favourably, therefore provide greater shareholder value but this is the way the world will no doubt be spinning a few years from now.

Truevalue Labs[48], who are set up to provide analytics for ESG investing. At the leading edge of ESG, Big Data and Artificial Intelligence (AI), they provide bespoke investment solutions so that clients can 'efficiently synthesise, analyse and derive insights from alternative data (and therefore) stand to gain a significant edge in the marketplace'.

We have arrived at the point now where the relentless financial crashes of boom and bust, coupled with a world full of inequalities, will mean greater policing and self-regulation of the markets, and that will not only be good for business but also good for humanity

It makes me wonder:

What if work was a construct that became more social, in that more humans start to choose the businesses they want to affiliate themselves with?

What if there was an index that reported on how successful the business was, how much it gives back to the world and how great it is to work there?

What if all businesses were made to declare an interest in social philanthropy and were incentivised and supported by their government and measured and audited on the work they did?

What if, as a result of COVID, we do nothing, and our world settles back to its normal economic, social and political rhythms?

It is predicted that 40% of the world's jobs in 15 years could be replaced by Artificial Intelligence (AI). What will this mean for global employment? How can we adapt? Could we look to be developing the capabilities of individuals to work in other future-focused sectors such as renewable energy?[49]

As leaders, we need to be holding conversations on these topics. We need to build more collaborative networks across the global leadership community and create opportunities for them to overcome many of the wider problems we face. We need to be looking beyond the spreadsheet and beyond the school gates, into the world in which we are creating. Is it a world where your legacy as a leader will nourish others and therefore sustain you? Will *you,* in the winter years of your life, be able to look back, and with a sense of pride see what you have done and the way you have done it in business as an act of kindness to humanity?

> They say there are two challenges to writing a book: starting it and finishing it.

In an attempt to conclude, I started to re-consider why I wanted to write this book in the first place. Initially I wanted to write a book on leadership and our human needs. That was the start point but I soon became gripped by the view that work itself and how businesses create work could be so much more than it is now. Then I was left with the dreaded question - so what? And along with it, the dreaded feeling of, who am I to challenge the norm? I am guessing this is quite normal, but I am very nervous about how this book will be received. How you will view me. I am hoping that the fact you have come this far and have stayed with me that you are thinking about 'what now?'. I know this book has some strong views that some will rightly challenge or disregard, it also has some views that could be viewed as too utopian, but I am still left with a view that work needs to do more for humanity. Work needs to be better and for it to be better we need better leadership, that was when I thought about the club!

- What if there was an online club where you could share stories of leadership that lifted humanity by meeting *its* needs?
- What if the purpose of this club were to develop leaders to meet the human needs of work *and* help spread the positive impact businesses can have in the world in which they operate?
- What if, when you joined this club, you could write and share your own leadership oath?
- And finally, what if, together, we created a cause for good, where through leadership at work, we built a better world?

Please join us by visiting:

Instagram: the.humanityclub

Twitter: @myhumanityclub

LinkedIn: linkedin.com/in/stevechurst

References

[1] https://www.forbes.com/sites/timothyjmcclimon/2020/01/16/corporate-giving-by-the-numbers/?sh=392beba26c51

[2] https://www.oecd.org/finance/ESG-Investing-Practices-Progress-Challenges.pdf

[3] https://www.studyfinds.org/modern-family-average-parent-spends-just-5-hours-face-to-face-with-their-kids-per-week/

[4] https://www.studyfinds.org/american-families-spend-37-minutes-quality-time/

[5] https://www.wateraid.org/facts-and-statistics#:~:text=1%20in%2010%20don't,millions%20more%20lives%20for%20good

[6] https://en.wikipedia.org/wiki/List_of_rail_accidents_in_the_United_Kingdom

It was four years after the privatisation of the UK Rail industry (1995) that there were a spate of headline rail crashes; September 1997 Southall 6 killed 150 injured, October 1999 Paddington 31 killed 523 injured, October 2000. Hatfield. 4 killed. 70+ injured, May 2002 Potters Bar 7 killed 76 injured. In fact, since privatisation in 1995 to 2008 a total of 82 people was killed and over a 1,318 were injured on UK rail networks.

It was the Grayrigg crash that peaked my interest in these statistics because 1 person was killed and 88 were injured. The Grayrigg derailment was a fatal railway accident that occurred at approximately 20:15 GMT on 23 February 2007, just to the south of Grayrigg, Cumbria, in the North West England. The 17:30 Virgin West Coast Pendolino West Coast Main Line InterCity service from London Euston to Glasgow Central derailed at 20:15 at a faulty set of points almost immediately after crossing the Docker Viaduct. Investigations were launched by the Rail Accident Investigation Branch and Her Majesty's Railway Inspectorate. RMT rail union leader Bob Crow said on BBC News that a points failure was responsible for the incident. Experts compared the cause to that of the Potters Bar rail crash in 2002. On 13 January 2012, the Office of Rail Regulation announced that Network Rail was to be prosecuted under Section 3(1) of the Health and Safety at Work Act 1974 for "the company's failure to provide and implement suitable and sufficient standards, procedures, guidance, training, tools and resources for the inspection and maintenance of fixed stretcher bar points".

[7] https://www.jimcollins.com/concepts/level-five-leadership.html

[8] Isolation and not listening to others causes leaders to make mistakes – out of touch etc

[9] https://www.forbes.com/sites/avivahwittenbergcox/2020/04/13/what-do-countries-with-the-best-coronavirus-reponses-have-in-common-women-leaders/#23259f253dec

[10] https://en.wikipedia.org/wiki/Knowledge_economy

[11] https://www.pbs.org/wgbh/pages/frontline/shows/walmart/secrets/barcode.html

[12] https://www.hse.gov.uk/statistics/dayslost.htm - HSE report 2018/19

[13] https://www.dailymail.co.uk/news/article-1019685/Workers-face-lie-detector-test-phone-tell-boss-pulling-sickie.html - Steve Doughty Daily Mail 14th May 2014

[14] https://www.apa.org/news/press/releases/2007/10/stress

[15] UK Times Saturday 8th October 2011. Article 'Business is not 'good' and 'bad'…but it must change.'

[16] https://www.goldmansachs.com/our-commitments/diversity-and-inclusion/racial--equity/index.html

[17] https://www.forbes.com/sites/vickyvalet/2019/09/17/the-worlds-most-reputable-companies-for-corporate-responsibility-2019/#51f082f0679b

[18] https://www.gilead.com/

[19] https://corpgov.law.harvard.edu/2018/07/20/the-boards-role-in-corporate-social-purpose/ - Posted by Amy Silverstein, Debbie McCormack, and Bob Lamm, Deloitte LLP

[20] https://www.conecomm.com/news-blog/2017/5/15/americans-willing-to-buy-or-boycott-companies-based-on-corporate-values-according-to-new-research-by-cone-communications

[21] https://www.bvt.org.uk/our-business/the-bournville-story/

[22] https://www.biography.com/business-figure/andrew-carnegie

[23] https://www.furninfo.com/furniture-world-articles/3859#:~:text=%E2%80%9CThat%20is%20the%20strategic%20opportunity,can%20make%20a%20huge%20difference.%E2%80%9D&text=%E2%80%9CFind%20your%20passion%20in%20your%20community.

[24] https://www.mercedesamgf1.com/en/news/2020/04/ucl-uclh-f1-project-pitlane-start-delivery-breathing-aids-nhs-hospitals/

[25] https://en.wikipedia.org/wiki/Malcolm_Baldrige_National_Quality_Award

[26] https://www.pro-development.co.uk/lack-of-investment-in-developing-managers-and-leaders/

[27] An unpredictable or unforeseen event, typically one with extreme consequences

[28] One example would be to offer employment for military veterans on a short term basis to give them the skills to adapt to civilian life

[29] https://www.england.nhs.uk/2020/04/jump-in-nhs-job-applications-as-public-back-coronavirus-battle/

[30] https://www.mindtools.com/pages/article/newSTR_90.htm - From Fundamentals of Strategy by G. Johnson, R. Whittington, and K. Scholes. Published by Pearson Education, 2012.

[31] 'Not only are attempts to script culture change doomed to failure, the attempt to manage culture tends to be seen as unethical, a threat to individual liberty.' Barratt (1992)

[32] https://en.wikipedia.org/wiki/Steve_Ballmer

[33] https://www.businessinsider.com/satya-nadella-microsoft-mindset-book-2019-1?r=US&IR=T

[34] https://hbr.org/2019/02/the-surprising-power-of-simply-asking-coworkers-how-theyre-doing

[35] https://www.mckinsey.com/featured-insights/gender-equality/focusing-on-what-works-for-workplace-diversity

[36] https://hbr.org/2018/03/americas-loneliest-workers-according-to-research

[37] https://assets.publishing.service.gov.uk/government/uploads/system/uploads/attachment_data/file/658145/thriving-at-work-stevenson-farmer-review.pdf

[38] Ren D, Wesselmann ED, Williams KD. Hurt people hurt people: ostracism and aggression. Curr Opin Psychol. 2018;19:34-38. doi:10.1016/j.copsyc.2017.03.026

[39] Guardian interview by Alex Hearn 12th March 2019 https://www.theguardian.com/technology/2019/mar/12/tim-berners-lee-on-30-years-of-the-web-if-we-dream-a-little-we-can-get-the-web-we-want

[40] People who fall under either antisocial, narcissistic, autism or schizophrenia have empathy impairments

[41] https://www.edelman.com/sites/g/files/aatuss191/files/2021-03/2021%20Edelman%20Trust%20Barometer.pdf

[42] https://en.wikipedia.org/wiki/Democracy_Index

[43] https://www.theregister.com/2020/07/06/oracle_lawsuit/

[44] https://www.sandiegouniontribune.com/business/story/2020-07-21/qualcomms-corporate-board-sued-for-lack-of-diversity-failure-to-appoint-black-director

[45] https://en.wikipedia.org/wiki/UK_Corporate_Governance_Code#Section_A:_Leadership

[46] https://www.frc.org.uk/directors/corporate-governance-and-stewardship/uk-corporate-governance-code/history-of-the-uk-corporate-governance-code

[47] https://justcapital.com/mission-impact/

[48] https://truvaluelabs.com/about

[49] This sector has taken a reduction in growth due to C-19 and the delay in construction

Printed in Great Britain
by Amazon